T5-DHA-842

The Crisis of Communism: Its Meaning, Origins, and Phases

Rett R. Ludwikowski

WITHDRAWN

STAFFORD LIBRARY
COLU...
1001 ROGE...
COLUMBIA, MO ...

Foreign Policy Report
1986

A Publication of the
INSTITUTE FOR FOREIGN POLICY ANALYSIS, INC.
Cambridge, Massachusetts, and Washington, D.C.

PERGAMON·BRASSEY'S
International Defense Publishers

Washington New York Oxford Toronto Sydney Frankfurt

335. 430947
L966C

Pergamon Press Offices:

U.S.A. Pergamon-Brassey's International Defense Publishers,
1340 Old Chain Bridge Road, McLean, Virginia, 22101, U.S.A.

Pergamon Press Inc., Maxwell House, Fairview Park,
Elmsford, New York 10523, U.S.A.

U.K. Pergamon Press Ltd., Headington Hill Hall,
Oxford OX3 0BW, England

CANADA Pergamon Press Canada Ltd., Suite 104, 150 Consumers Road,
Willowdale, Ontario M2J 1P9, Canada

AUSTRALIA Pergamon Press (Aust.) Pty. Ltd., P.O. Box 544,
Potts Point, NSW 2011, Australia

FEDERAL REPUBLIC Pergamon Press GmbH, Hammerweg 6,
OF GERMANY D-6242 Kronberg-Taunus, Federal Republic of Germany

BRAZIL Pergamon Editora Ltda., Rua Eça de Queiros, 346,
CEP 04011, São Paulo, Brazil

JAPAN Pergamon Press Ltd., 8th Floor, Matsuoka Central Building,
1-7-1 Nishishinjuku, Shinjuku, Tokyo 160, Japan

PEOPLE'S REPUBLIC Pergamon Press, Qianmen Hotel, Beijing,
OF CHINA People's Republic of China

Copyright© 1986 Pergamon Press, Inc.

*All rights reserved. No part of this publication may be reproduced,
stored in a retrieval system or transmitted in any form or by any
means: electronic, electrostatic, magnetic tape, mechanical,
photocopying, recording or otherwise, without permission in writing
from the publishers.*

First Printing 1986

Library of Congress Cataloging-in-Publication Data

Ludwikowski, Rett R.
The crisis of communism.

(Foreign policy report) (Special report)
"A Publication of the Institute for Foreign Policy
Analysis, Inc."
1. Communism—Soviet Union. 2. Soviet Union—
Economic conditions—1976-. 3. Soviet Union—Politics and
government—1982-. 4. Soviet Union—Social conditions—
1970-. I. Institute for Foreign Policy Analysis. II. Title. III.
Series. IV. Series: Special report (Institute for Foreign
Policy Analysis)
HX313.5.L83   1986   335.43'0947   86-20519
ISBN 0-08-034496-8 (pbk.)

Printed by Corporate Press, Inc., Washington, D.C.

To Russell
Archduke of Mecosta
and Annette
Princess of All Lands,
to whose friendship
I owe the most precious
thing for me,
freedom.

"The cause of the Party's defectiveness must be found. All our principles were right, but our results were wrong. . . . Our will was hard and pure, we should have been loved by the people. But they hate us. Why are we so odious and detested?

"We brought you truth, and in our mouth it sounded a lie. We brought you freedom, and it looks in our hands like a whip. We brought you the living life, and where our voice is heard the trees wither and there is a rustling of dry leaves. We brought you the promise of the future, but our tongue stammered and barked. . . ."

Arthur Koestler
Darkness at Noon

Contents

Preface

Passing along a street in Cracow the day before I left Poland in 1982, I noticed a large inscription on the wall of a house: "Proletarians of all countries, forgive me—Karl Marx."

That inscription symbolized the opposition of most Poles to communism, and ridiculed party propaganda which proclaimed the opposite. The apology on the wall brought to mind a question often put to me during my visit to the United States the previous summer: Will the crisis of communism begin in Poland? The sign on the wall seemed to be the answer.

The leaflet containing a cartoon strip stuck to the door of another house offered a similar reply. In the first box, Edward Gierek (the former First Secretary of the Communist Party in Poland), at the wheel of a ship, was asking workers in the background to aid the party. There was only one word at the bottom of the drawing: "Help!" In the second box, a worker was standing at the wheel, trying to help steer the ship, but Gierek was pulling the wheel in one direction and the worker in the opposite one. In the third box, the same worker, face to face with another high-ranking party member (who had replaced Gierek), was shaking his fist and shouting: "I don't give a damn about you."

If we were to assess the position of communism in Poland from the thousands of similar inscriptions and leaflets, we would have to acknowledge that the crisis of this system is a fact. On the other hand, the Soviet system has had a history of troubles and turbulence since 1917. So the question remains: What does this "crisis" signify? Will it be localized in Poland, or will it spread to the other countries of the Soviet bloc? Is it the result of temporary weakness, or of the continuing impotence of successive communist regimes? What are the roots of the crisis and what are the prospects for communism in the world? This book is dedicated to the consideration of these questions.

The idea for this book developed slowly during those years which the writer spent living under the communist regime. It always puzzled him that it was possible for the Bolsheviks, who even after the seizure of power were a small, unpopular minority, to remain in control of their gigantic empire. On the one hand, it was amazing to realize how effective the totalitarian machinery of power could be. On the other hand, it was fascinating to follow the inexorable breakdown of this machinery—to watch how the governmental structure, which was intended to be so flexible, and the means of total social control, which were to be employed only temporarily, had gradually undergone a process of fossilization. The total dedication of the leaders of the totalitarian state to one aim—revolution and post-revolutionary survival—shattered the capability of the system to reform or rejuvenate itself. The mechanisms which initially strengthened the power of the ruling communist elite began to break down. It was increasingly obvious that the process of their deterioration was irreversible.

For someone who lived so long under a communist regime, it is quite amazing to discover how little understanding of the crisis of communism there is in the West, and how strong the communist system appears to be to Western observers who still can detect only occasional periods of "distortions" and "temporary weakness." The West is still inclined to view the Soviet system only in terms of its gigantic military potential, and to underestimate its internal economic, moral, social, and ideological failures and decay. Soviet propaganda, which continuously produces new visions of the "glorious Soviet past and victorious future," is still successful in the West. As a Polish proverb says: "Under communism only the future is certain: the past is always changing." So let us examine this "flexible" past and draw a few conclusions about the "predetermined" future of communism.

There are many people to whom the author of this book is indebted, and I am particularly conscious that without the assistance of my American friends this book would never have been written. I am grateful to Dr. Russell Kirk and Annette Kirk, who assisted me continually after my departure from Poland. To their friendship I owe much of whatever I might contribute to the field of communist studies. I would also like to express my special gratitude to Dr. Milorad Drachkovitch and Professor Wenceslas J. Wagner whose expert comments and personal encouragement were invaluable to me. I owe a special measure of thanks to the Hoover Institution on War, Revolution and Peace, and to the Marguerite Eyer Wilbur Foundation, which were co-sponsors of this study, and to the Columbus School of Law at The Catholic University of America, where the manuscript was completed and edited. I am especially indebted to Professor Steven P. Frankino, Dean of the Columbus School of Law, and to Mr. Richard T. Burres, Chairman of the Publication Committee and Associate Director of the Hoover Institution, for their most generous assistance. Association with various scholars of these institutions has been a source of continual stimulation to me. I would also like to thank the personnel of the Hoover Institution Library and the assistants of Dr. Russell Kirk for their help in my research. Mr. Joseph D. Dwayer, Mrs. Maria Teutsch-Dwyer, Mr. Joseph Baldacchino, and Ms. Lauren Bloom have been most helpful in the editing of this book, and I wish to express my thanks for their time and assistance. Finally, I would like to express my deep appreciation to my wife and my children who indulgently tolerated the weekends which I spent working in my office.

Rett R. Ludwikowski
Professor of Law
The Catholic University of America

Summary Overview

During the past year the Western press has given a lot of publicity to the new attempts at economic reform in the Soviet Union. In his interview for *Time* magazine, Mikhail Gorbachev stated that "large-scale economic experiments are underway aimed essentially at developing a more efficient mechanism of management that would dramatically accelerate the rate of scientific and technological progress and make better use of all resources." The widespread expectation in the West that Gorbachev's reform efforts might achieve some success was based on Gorbachev's vigor and determination, on the fact that he is the youngest Soviet leader since Malenkov to attain the position of Secretary General of the Communist Party of the Soviet Union, as well as the youngest of his colleagues in the Soviet Politburo.

The more cautious commentators remind us that Yuri Andropov, in his first major policy address, also freely acknowledged that the previous period had not solved the Soviet bloc's most urgent problems and declared that he would fight against inefficiency in agriculture, drunkenness, corruption, the black market, the general disintegration of the communist economy, and so forth. Others pointed out that Andropov's predecessors had made similar pledges when first addressing the Central Committee.

In 1982 the West's optimistic assessment of the "new era of Soviet reforms" stemmed from tales about Andropov's predilections for jazz, whisky, and Western novels. Now it is based on the fact that Gorbachev is "a man of a new generation," on his expertise in agriculture, and on reports from his visits in Western Europe where he was portrayed as "a civilized diplomat" with a sense of humor, able to absorb the new concepts of government and science.

At the 27th Soviet Party Congress Gorbachev talked again about the need for speeding economic growth and called for "openness" in public life. The Chernobyl accident, however, challenged his credibility in the West, and the American press again began to question why, despite all repeated optimistic prognoses, nothing has changed substantially in the Soviet economy since Khrushchev. After decades of economic failures, the West still seems surprised that the communist system remains so resistant to change.

The author of this book believes that it is time to realize that Soviet communism is in crisis. Despite all the talk about "radical reform," nothing can hide this reality. True, the system has not collapsed, but also, until recently, it has not shown any signs of a quick economic recovery. The shift of succession to the younger generation may result in attempts to introduce a new epoch of modest reforms. It is even very likely that economic stagnation will compel Gorbachev to resume attempts to overhaul the Soviet economy. Yet, the success of any reform movement will depend on many factors—social, ideological, economic, political. The personal characteristics of Soviet leaders and their awareness of the deficiencies of the system will not be enough to provide the solution. With regard to carrying out a major reconstruction, not a marginal modification, the economically counter-productive elements of the system are more significant. They have worked, and most probably will continue to work, against any attempt at reform.

A substantial recovery of the socialist economy is not likely to occur for a variety of reasons:

(1) The system has forever destroyed the "collective mentality" which was to be a basic component of communist political culture.

(2) The crisis of communist ideology is irreversible.

(3) The ideological crisis has undermined the rudiments of communist morality and corroded all Marxist-Leninist values, including the key dogma of common ownership.

(4) The moral and ideological crisis has deprived workers and managers of their incentive to work.

(5) Without the rudiments of democracy, people can be forced to work but they will not work efficiently. Yet democratic transformations are too dangerous for the ruling elite; they are simply incompatible with the system's totalitarian framework.

(6) The double standard of morality, together with massive economic dislocations, has created a black market and corruption, which have been tolerated for so long that they are now irrevocably integrated into the way of life in communist countries.

(7) The need for creating a relatively open party elite forced the party to build a system of "negative selection" that promotes compliant, conform-able "yes-men" who care more about their careers than about the system of communist values.

(8) Incompetence, widespread corruption, and the unaccountability of decisionmakers are incompatible with the basic principles of economic effi-ciency.

(9) Lack of information about, coordination of, and proper control over the implementation of production decisions, coupled with a form of decen-tralization that is more apparent than real, have crippled the socialist system of central planning and decisionmaking.

(10) Without the party bureaucracy and *nomenklatura* system, the party cannot function; but with them, no reform is possible. Both are key ingre-dients of a system which can be overturned but not reformed. They are an inseparable part of communist totalitarianism.

The word "crisis" is not used here to indicate that the Soviet Union is on the verge of imminent collapse or that it has entered a crucial period in which a political upheaval is impending. Rather, "crisis" is used to signify that Soviet economic failure has undermined the basic structure of Soviet totalitarianism and that the Soviet economic system has reached a decisive turn from which there is no retreat.

To understand the possible consequences of this situation it is necessary not only to comprehend the meaning and significance of the crisis, but also to examine its origins and stages. The crisis began when Lenin implemented Marx's ideas in so underdeveloped a country as the Russia of World War I. It has unfolded during the periods of Stalin's purges, the revisionism of Khrushchev's era, and Soviet interventions in Hungary, Czechoslovakia, and Afghanistan; and it has most recently manifested itself in the Polish turbulence of the 1980s.

The crucial symptom signifying the corroding effects of the crisis is the growing awareness in Soviet bloc societies that the crisis is real and its consequences are irreversible. There is an increasing recognition of the complexity of factors which contribute to the economic, ideological, moral, and social fallacies of the system and its permanent weakness. The realization that these defects are irremediable and reside in the inherent nature of the system multiplies the symptoms of the crisis, deprives the people of incentives to work, and reduces the group of activists and believers emotionally dedicated to communism.

There is no question that communist regimes still control the several Soviet bloc countries. However, the strategies used to maintain this control are gradually being undermined by the crisis. More and more the communist empire rests solely on one pillar—the military/secret police apparatus—while the others are being corroded and are less and less able to support the whole structure. Bare military power can for some time keep societies under control, but it cannot serve as the catalyst of successful development. Societies deprived of moral strength and perspectives of economic and social progress cannot keep up with the more prosperous free societies of the world.

Mikhail Gorbachev is confronted with the question that is undoubtedly provoking internal debate in the Soviet hierarchy: Whether to go on arming at the expense of the faltering economy, or to restructure a less restrictive social and economic system at the cost of possibly losing nuclear and missile supremacy. He faces a serious dilemma: The reconstruction process could lead to a real and dramatic recovery, but it could also imperil the totalitarian foundation of the state by relaxing the Communist Party's grip on Soviet life. The Soviet leaders realize that in this situation the well-tested policy of detente and cooperation might again offer a more promising solution. A renewal of the spirit of detente might speed up the inflow of Western technology and capital to the Soviet bloc and enable the Soviet Union to maintain at least strategic parity with the United States without experiencing a further decline in the rate of growth of consumption and productivity or making risky social concessions.

This strategy, however, might be undermined by the internal crisis depicted above. This crisis, even if it does not directly affect the Soviet machinery of totalitarian control, might reduce chances for successful implementation of the detente policy. The repeated application of terror unaccompanied by policies designed to mollify the societies of the bloc countries by nationalistic, ideological, or economic stimulants might result in the deterioration of relations with the West and the consequent weakening of the Soviet military posture. The paradox of communism is that without totalitarian methods, the system can hardly survive; but with them, its rotten foundations cannot be restructured. Totalitarianism is a weapon that cuts both ways: it defends the ruling bureaucratic party elite, but, on the other hand, undermines the pillars on which the power of this elite is based. The moment of final "collapse" of the communist system cannot be precisely determined, but it seems quite certain that, despite the heralded reforms, the differences in economic progress and social cohesion between the nations of the West and the Soviet bloc countries will grow wider in the second half of the 1980s.

1.
Where is the Crisis of Communism?

IN THE MIDDLE of the 1950s, Western anxiety about the Soviet bloc was compounded by a grudging admiration for the Stalinist industrial revolution. As Isaac Deutscher wrote, "In the present decade Russia is beginning to overtake the combined industrial power of Germany, France and Great Britain; and she obviously aspires to catching up with the United States in the not too remote future."[1] Western panic reached its climax when the first Sputnik was launched and Nikita Khrushchev announced that, by the late 1970s, the Soviet Union would surpass the strongest capitalist countries in production per capita. Even the level of consumer goods available to the Russian population was to be higher than that of the United States.

By the mid-1960s, however, the prospects of the communist economy were already being downgraded from the level heralded by Soviet propaganda. By the late 1970s the economic decay of the entire bloc was no longer open to question. Indeed, some of the "people's democracies," with Poland at the head, were on the verge of total economic collapse. Shortages of the most basic commodities, galloping inflation, currency devaluation, debt to the verge of insolvency, inefficiency in agriculture, disproportionate development between the industrial and agricultural sectors, massive waste caused by shortages of materials and spare parts, heavy reliance on coal-centered industry that was technologically obsolete, lack of organizational ability—problems such as these were observable to varying degrees in all of the communist countries. Yuri Andropov, in 1982, in his first major policy address as General Secretary of the Communist Party of the Soviet Union (CPSU), freely acknowledged that efforts in the previous period had not solved the Soviet bloc's most urgent economic problems.[2] Awareness of the problem also was growing in the West. "A few years ago," wrote Marshall I. Goldman,

Soviet prospects looked far more promising to me. When American sovietologists painted a picture of the Soviet Union showing it on the verge of doom, if not collapse, I invariably responded that they were viewing something radically different from what I knew. Now I am not so sure. Conditions in the Soviet Union

---

[1] Isaac Deutscher, *Russia After Stalin* (London: Hamish Hamilton, 1953), pp. 58-59.
[2] See Martin Ebon, *The Andropov File* (New York: McGraw-Hill, 1983), p. 240.

deteriorated significantly, and it will take some skill and wise leadership to find a safe course.[3]

Despite such observations, Western governments continued to release periodic reports reminding the public that Soviet economic potential should not be underestimated. During the last 30 years, we learned, Soviet industrial output had increased sevenfold, agricultural production had doubled, gross national product had quadrupled, and consumption per capita had tripled.[4] Even as recently as 1982 (almost concurrently with Andropov's speech), the American news media captured the public's attention with the details of a CIA report released by the Joint Economic Committee of the Congress. "The Soviet Union has experienced steady economic development and improving standards of living over the past 30 years," said the Committee's Chairman, Democrat Henry Reuss. "The annual rate of increase in Soviet military expenditures—4 percent to 5 percent—has not accelerated over the past 15 years. The Soviet diet has improved greatly over the past 30 years. And in general despite 'problems' the USSR, far from being on the verge of economic collapse, has experienced major growth."[5]

Some scholars also denied that the state of affairs in the Soviet Union could be described as one of "crisis." In "Andropov and His Soviet Union," Alain Besancon wrote:

After sixty years of "impetuous growth," of "uninterrupted progress," the average Soviet wage is, in purchasing power, half as large as that of Brazil. A peasantry twice as numerous as the whole agricultural class of Western Europe and North America fails to feed the country adequately. Outside the military sector, the technological revolution has wholly failed. In sixty years the U.S.S.R. has not invented a medicine, a textile fiber, a plastic material, a saleable computer. It is one of the rare countries where, as Dr. Feshbach has shown, the rate of infant mortality increases and life expectancy in general diminishes. So: Is the U.S.S.R. in crisis? Not at all, because what we call a crisis is not a crisis for them.[6]

In 1985 the Western press gave a lot of publicity to the new attempts at economic reform in the Soviet Union. "Gorbachev Sets Shift in Economy," "Gorbachev's Vigor Holds Attention of Soviets," "Gorbachev Orders Wide 'Restructuring' of Soviet Economy"—these are the titles of only a few articles which examined Gorbachev's "breathtaking determination to make changes in the Soviet economy."[7]

The general optimism as to the chances of Gorbachev's reforms which accompanied these comments was based on Gorbachev's vigor, on the fact

---

[3] Marshall I. Goldman, *USSR in Crisis: The Failure of an Economic System* (New York: W.W. Norton & Company, 1983), p. xi.

[4] Ebon, *The Andropov File*, op. cit., p. 132; see also Goldman, op. cit., p. 174.

[5] "Doughnut and the Hole," *Wall Street Journal*, December 29, 1982.

[6] Alain Besancon, "Andropov and His Soviet Union," *Policy Review*, Summer 1983.

[7] *Washington Post*, March 12, June 4, 12, 16, 17, and 21, 1985.

that he is the youngest Soviet leader to attain the position of Secretary General of the Communist Party of the Soviet Union since Malenkov,[8] and recently was the youngest of his colleagues in the Soviet Politburo. Gorbachev is also the first leader since Lenin to have completed regular higher education, and his dedication to the reform of the Soviet economy was proved in the summer of 1981 when he and his supporters tried to defend a radical reform of Soviet agriculture which would have had the effect of excluding some sectors of agriculture from the system of central planning.[9] The reform was never implemented because of opposition from the conservative group in the Politburo (supported by Brezhnev and Prime Minister Tikhonov), but Gorbachev made his mark as a reformer.

The American public may inquire with good reason: Who is finally right in these evaluations? Which opinions are more reliable—those of Andropov and other Soviet leaders, who from time to time have admitted the shortcomings of the Soviet economy, or those of the Western mass media, which tend most often to stress Soviet economic achievements? I have often been asked by my confused students: Is there a genuine crisis, or are the troubles in the Soviet bloc countries only temporary ones that can be easily overcome in the future? In short, is there a crisis?

A careful examination reveals several beliefs which adherents of both sides of the argument tend to hold in common. First, both sides agree that Soviet "achievements" have often been exaggerated by the Western news media. Before we admire the first great industrial boom in the Soviet Union, it is important to remember how superficial it was. Too often, Communist Party leaders were interested in making spectacular technical advances that were to be achieved irrespective of the costs. As Khrushchev himself acknowledged: "We have designed the first artificial earth satellite, but we have not reached the stage of replacing crowbars and spades with machines."[10] The emphasis placed by Soviet leaders on rapid industrialization frequently disrupted the long-term pattern of investment. Discriminatory overallocation of resources to heavy industry, together with comparative neglect of light industry and agriculture, inflicted serious harm on cooperation between the various sectors of the economy. While the greatest burdens of industrialization were borne by the peasantry, which provided manpower for the new industries, society at large also paid a steep price in the form of a sharp decline in the standard of living.[11] Collectivization, which was supposed to

---

[8] Lenin, when he reached this position, was 47, Stalin 50, Malenkov 51, Khrushchev 59, Brezhnev 58, Andropov 68, Chernenko 71.

[9] See Arnold Beichman and Mikhail S. Bernstam, *Andropov, New Challenge to the West* (New York: Stein and Day, 1983), pp. 198-208.

[10] Cited by Robert Conquest in *Common Sense About Russia* (London: Gollancz, 1960), p. 34.

[11] For more detailed figures, see G. Warren Nutter, "The Soviet Economy: Retrospect and Prospect," in Milorad Drachkovitch, editor, *Fifty Years of Communism in Russia* (University Park, Pa.: Pennsylvania State University Press, 1968), pp. 73-98.

increase the efficiency of agriculture and was accomplished at great human cost, proved to be an utter failure. Soviet economists have been faced with the fact that collective farms are much less productive, given the resources invested, than individual property devoted to agriculture. When using figures, therefore, we must keep in mind that the Soviet economy is full of paradoxes that are almost inconceivable to the people of the advanced countries of the West. Before allowing ourselves to be impressed by figures showing that Soviet agricultural production has doubled over the past three decades, we must remember that—as described in the report of the plenary meeting of the CPSU Central Committee in 1953, almost three decades ago—Khrushchev admitted that both the amount of grain per capita and the total number of cattle produced had declined to lower levels than in Tsarist times.[12] When mentioning the growth of national product, moreover, we must realize that the basic problem of the Soviet economy is one of quality, not quantity.[13] From an academic perspective, therefore, reports of Soviet economic "achievements" should be viewed with cool skepticism.

A second point about which those on both sides of the argument seem to agree is that the gap between Soviet economic capacity and that of the industrialized countries of the West has been getting wider, rather than narrower, in recent decades. This does not mean that Soviet economic potential is permanently diminishing. Indeed, the potential of the Soviet economy, as measured by the quantity of natural and human resources at its command, is quite large and should not be underestimated. Rather, the source of the Soviet Union's economic distress is to be found in anomalies of development: in a gigantic disproportion, for example, between the amount of capital invested and the value of the resulting production, and in a chaotic absence of cooperation among the myriad segments of the economy. Hence we can observe the "growth" of Soviet economic potential, measured statistically, while simultaneously witnessing a genuine disintegration of the communist economy which in certain parts of the Soviet Union has assumed catastrophic proportions.

A third point on which there is common agreement is that the Soviet Union remains a military superpower. While economic inefficiency has slowed the rate of growth in military spending from what it might otherwise have been, it has not undermined the core of Soviet military might. This

---

[12] See Conquest, *Common Sense About Russia*, op. cit., p. 50. We can argue that the "daily calorie intake of the Soviet citizenry is equal to that of U.S. citizens." Yet, at the same time, we must remember what the structure of consumption is in the Soviet Union—that, for example, the current average per capita annual intake of meat in the Soviet Union is some 56 kilograms, while the U.S. average intake is over 100. See Roy D. Laird, "A New Era in Soviet Agriculture," in Donald R. Kelley, editor, *Soviet Politics in the Brezhnev Era* (New York: Praeger, 1980), p. 59. For more detailed figures, see N. Laguton, *Ekonomika Selskogo Khozjaistva*, No. 3, March 1975, pp. 97-104.

[13] See George E. Feiwel, "Economic Performance and Reforms in the Soviet Union," in Kelley, editor, *Soviet Politics in the Brezhnev Era*, op. cit., p. 101.

means that, whether we choose to apply the term "crisis" to the Soviet situation or not, we cannot expect economic problems alone to lead to any fundamental change in the nature of the Soviet regime in the near future.

Controversies over the "crisis of communism" focus on two main issues: the capacity of the Soviet system for reform, and the extent to which recent Soviet economic troubles may undermine the pillars of the communist totalitarian order.

Scholars who are inclined to stress the "crisis" of the communist economy hold that the Soviet system has reached a crucial state of affairs from which there is no retreat. While agreeing by and large that a collapse is not necessarily imminent, these scholars believe that the Soviet system has begun a process of deterioration which, though it might be prolonged, cannot be reversed. According to this view, the Soviet bloc will not be able to keep up with the West, as was promised in the 1950s. And for the Soviet leaders, this failure to "step forward" will have the impact of "two steps backward." Public disappointment may lead to turbulence in the subjugated countries. Although increasing the prosperity or standard of living of the masses is by no means the main goal of the Soviet government, the communist leaders must nevertheless be concerned that repeated manifestations of public dissatisfaction could limit the state's ability to penetrate all spheres of social life. The Polish challenge to the Soviet system may prove not to have been exceptional. If so, it could become necessary—in order to maintain full military control over the Soviet bloc, monopoly control of all means of communication and education, and complete control of the economic activities of its citizens—for the state to return to Stalinist methods of personal repression. Yet resumption of Stalinist terror could well result in the loss of Western credits and the total collapse of detente. The lack of Western subsidization could in turn diminish the chances of final victory in the arms race, endangering the continuance of military superiority. In this way the economic crisis might hamper the achievement of the "true socialist aim": the extension of the control of the Soviet Communist Party over the entire world. In the future, it could threaten the basis of the communist empire.

The critics of this approach argue that the Soviet regime has had a history of troubles and at least some degree of turbulence since 1917. But, they say, the usual experience has been that, as communism suffered setbacks in one sphere, its influence grew in another. At the same time, there has been a general tendency in the West to overestimate the vulnerability of the communist system. While Western scholars have written volumes about the "crisis" from this perspective, they have failed to provide explicit backing for their belief that the disintegration of the communist economy was irreversible.

Let me clarify my own view. If the word "crisis" is used to indicate that the Soviet Union is on the verge of imminent collapse or that it has entered a crucial time in which a political upheaval is impending, then I must be numbered among the opponents of this theory, as I do not anticipate the collapse of the communist system in the near future. On the other hand, if the term "crisis" is meant to signify that Soviet economic failure has undermined the basic structure of Soviet totalitarianism and that the Soviet economic system has reached a decisive turn from which there is no retreat, I would agree that the Soviet regime has entered a period of "crisis."

Is the communist economy capable of reform? This question is constantly raised, and my reply is definitely in the negative. While the communist economy may be subject to some marginal modifications, any substantive reconstruction would require a fundamental change of the whole political and economic structure.

Among the key elements that characterize the socialist economy are the following: (1) Socialist ownership of productive resources in the form of state property. (2) Income redistribution controlled by the government. (3) The principle of central planning. (4) The principle of "democratic centralism," which in the economic sphere combines a centralized decision-making process with dependence on the creative activity and initiative of local managers.

The simplest explanation of the factors militating against any fundamental reform of the communist system is that all four of the above basic characteristics of communism are economically counterproductive. The economic fallacies of communism are implicit in the system itself, hence cannot be uprooted without destroying the communist system.

While the crisis of communism has been at the center of much discussion, a number of important points often have been overlooked. One deficiency in the usual treatment of this issue is that the crisis is seen as almost exclusively an economic affair. In fact, the crisis encompasses not only worsening and irreparable economic dislocations but also an irreversible deterioration of public morality, a breakdown of confidence in the communist leadership, and a growing distrust of the basic tenets of communist ideology. Thus, the crisis can be fully comprehended only as the consequence of the interaction of various economic, social, moral, and ideological elements. When we discuss the crisis of communism, all of these factors must be taken into account.

What Happened to the Communist "Collective Mentality"?

The Constitution of the USSR says that state property—the principal form of socialist property—is subject to common ownership by the Soviet people (Article 11). Soviet citizens are obliged to preserve and protect socialist property (Article 61). According to Marxism-Leninism, respect for collective values was to follow from the growing unity of individual and society. Socialist doctrine promoted the ideas of ultimate equality, freedom, and justice, and offered a belief that these goals could be accomplished only by a total reconciliation between individual and social interests. Awareness of the superiority of shared interest to that of individual interest was supposed to create a "collective mentality"—a precondition for the further evolution of the society toward communism. On behalf of the collective interest, not only all means of production and distribution but social, moral, and even religious convictions were to be subject to public control. The individual's rights and duties were to be determined by society.

The attempt to create a "collective mentality" turned out to be a total failure. The concept, which in a way typified the Old Bolsheviks, fell victim to corrosion in the decades of Stalin's rule. The fact that millions of people were encouraged, and even forced, to survive at the cost of others' lives could not help but drastically affect public morality. The role of the collective in the formation of a socialist personality was severely crippled. In fact, party propaganda notwithstanding, the collective in any true sense posed a threat to totalitarian control. The real aim of the collective, as it developed under Stalin, was not to bring people together, but to serve as an instrument for the destruction of the individual approach to life, and to promote the complete atomization of society. Artificial communities created by the state were to destroy all genuine intermediate social structures. The destruction of all trust in mutual relations between people, the disintegration of family loyalty, and the denunciation of parents by their children were intended to weaken the distinction between truth and falsehood and to deprive individuals of the capacity to form their own opinions. Religious beliefs were proclaimed to be in clear contradiction to the anti-materialistic philosophy of communism. The moral impact of the Church was blocked, but was never replaced by any kind of communist morality. Socialist collectives, which had been expected to replace the Church's authority, never gained broad public respect.

The Bolshevization of society resulted in its cultural and moral impoverishment, in the leveling of all groups to the lowest common denominator. "Social justice," comprehended in this way, led in practice to the total subordination of private interests to some projection of "public good," which was usually offered by a relatively small group of social leaders who only pretended to speak on behalf of society as a whole. The total unity between individual and society appeared to be nothing but a total destruction of human individuality.

It has often been argued that, in the end, the millions of slave laborers under Stalin achieved remarkable results. According to this view, the system of compulsive labor played an important economic role and was not as inefficient as usually assumed.[14] But the calculation is not so simple. Over-looked by proponents of this view are the far-reaching consequences of the system of compulsive work. In reality, Stalinist economic adventurism stifled the initiative of workers and their incentive to be truly productive in a way that was to last for decades. Communist enterprises based on compulsive labor produced goods at the cost of a maximum expenditure of resources. The reduction of such expenditures was made impossible by the lack of any true incentive to achieve more efficient production. Even in the period of de-Stalinization, when the labor camps were reduced, the far-reaching consequences of the system were perceptible. The effects could be seen in extraordinarily low labor discipline, hooliganism, drunkenness, bribe-taking, a dual standard of morality between Soviet workers and the technical intelligentsia, neglect of equipment, absenteeism, and a destructive trend called "steal-and-let-others-steal"—all of which are habits deeply rooted in the Soviet labor system. From this perspective, the method of compulsive work proved to be an unmitigated disaster.

When we discuss the difficulties of the Soviet economy, all of these factors must be taken into consideration. It is certainly true that some of the losses suffered by the communist economy during Stalin's time cannot be rectified. Any chance that communism might have had for building a communist morality was lost during that period. The people stopped identifying state ownership with their own interests in property. They ceased to believe in the just redistribution of income controlled by the government. The communist state lost forever any chance of creating a "collective mentality"— a precondition for any successful development of a socialist economy.

Ideological and Moral Background of the Economic Crisis

The decay of communist ideology is undoubtedly a leitmotif of all debates over the crisis of the Soviet political system. Numerous commentators on Soviet domestic problems like to emphasize the total decomposition of Marxism-Leninism in the Soviet bloc. They argue that in today's Soviet bloc countries nobody takes ideological clichés seriously. Party leaders are cynical, and the public hates communism. As Vladimir Bukovsky has written: "From top to bottom, no one believes in Marxist dogma anymore, even though they continue to measure their actions by it, refer to it, and use it as a stick to beat one another with: it is both a proof of loyalty and a meal ticket."[15]

Some distinguished writers like Alexander Solzhenitsyn hold that Marxism-Leninism is a dead ideology in the sense that "even during its best

---

[14] Robert Conquest, *The Great Terror: Stalin's Purge of the Thirties* (New York: Macmillan, 1968), p. 357.

[15] Quoted in Donald D. Barry and Carol Barner-Barry, *Contemporary Soviet Politics: An Introduction* (Englewood Cliffs, N.J.: Prentice-Hall, 1982), p. 37.

decades it was totally mistaken in its predictions and was never a science." However, this completely false and harmful ideology is followed blindly by Soviet leaders. Their adherence to the precepts of Marxism-Leninism is a main source of the numerous failures and blunders of the Soviet regime. "The spiritual renaissance of our country," argues Solzhenitsyn, "lies in our liberation from this deadening, killing ideology."[16]

Some other writers, among whom Leszek Kolakowski is a prominent example, believe ideology is used in the Soviet bloc primarily as an instrument for legitimizing the power system. Kolakowski writes: "The socialist class of exploiters is not eager to retain and extend its power because it professes a false doctrine (after all, throughout history despots did quite well without Marxism); rather, they adhere to this doctrine as a tool to retain and extend their power."[17]

It is worth noting that discussion of the significance of communist ideology usually concentrates on the most recent symptoms of ideological crisis, while seldom if ever considering the economic and moral repercussions of ideological decay. This leaves an impression that the collapse of communist ideology is a relatively recent occurrence. In fact, the role played by Marxism-Leninism has undergone visible transformations throughout the duration of communist rule in Russia, and the ideological crisis has had much more extensive consequences than is usually recognized.

The Old Bolsheviks were masters of revolutionary techniques, but they had no experience in running a state. They knew how to subvert, destroy, and change, but had little knowledge of how to build, create, or introduce more advanced institutions, better economic techniques, or improved agricultural methods. For them Marxism served as a sort of sacred guide to be followed almost blindly. But experience usually is a better teacher than theories. The tenets of "genuine Marxism" often proved inapplicable in post-revolutionary Russia. Soon it appeared that the Bolshevik Party, despite its adherence to Marxism, did not practice its basic assumptions. On the one hand, the Bolsheviks had to pervert Marx's theory for their own purposes; on the other, they were not able to create a new theory. The solution hit upon was to appear to adhere to the basic dogmas of Marxism, while imposing strictly controlled thought. The bigger their pragmatic deviations, the stronger their pretensions to be the most orthodox followers of "scientific socialism." Marxism, or rather Marxism-Leninism (which means Lenin's Marxism), has never become a dead ideology. It played and still plays a significant role.

---

[16] Alexander Solzhenitsyn, *Warning to the West* (New York: Farrar, Straus and Giroux, 1976), p. 114.

[17] Leszek Kolakowski, "Ideology in Eastern Europe," in Milorad Drachkovitch, editor, *East Central Europe: Yesterday-Today-Tomorrow* (Stanford, Calif.: Hoover Institution Press, 1982), p. 45.

The theory of Marxism-Leninism is sufficiently flexible to provide general principles which can be adopted by the regime and exploited as its stable theoretical background. At the same time, no doctrinal tenets are sacrosanct under Soviet policy except insofar as they are useful to the ruling elite. As Daniel Bell has correctly pointed out, in the Soviet system "no single element of doctrine is a keystone whose removal would cause the collapse of Soviet ideology."[18] The regime armed with totalitarian machinery does not need a precise guide to its actions. What it does require is general confirmation that the leaders are moving in the correct direction; it needs a theoretical justification, and Marxism-Leninism is able to provide this disguise.

Does this mean that ideology no longer causes Soviet leaders to act? In a literal sense, the answer is yes. This does not mean, however, that the role played by ideology is meaningless. Marxism-Leninism long ago ceased to serve as the main guide to action, but it did not disappear. Though pragmatic Soviet leaders do not follow Marx's recommendations literally, the communist rulers are forced to decorate their decisions, speeches, and rhetoric with Marxist terminology. And this everyday contact with Marxist clichés and slogans has an inevitable impact on their mentality. After all, adherence to Marxism-Leninism can be a source of difficulty but it can also be very convenient. When at a loss for a solution to a policy question, party leaders can open the "sacred books" and find some "phrase" which, in the future, can justify even the most stupid decision. Obviously, in such a situation, mechanical application of Marxism can only exacerbate the consequences of the former inept policy, but the ideological facade is a useful weapon until such time as a stronger contestant is able to pin a "revisionist" label on such an interpretation. Viewed from the perspective of a Soviet leader, then, ideology can serve as a means of legitimization and de-legitimization of political, economic, and social decisions, an excellent weapon in political and internal struggles, and a justification of any international strategy. And, after all, it provides a stable theoretical background for the system.

Ideology has also played an important social role. Its unifying function—its role as a sort of "social cement"—has often been pointed out by Western political thinkers.[19] Ideology helped the ruling elite to maximize its control over the thinking and actions of individuals. It was a priceless method to mobilize public energy, an excellent instrument of political manipulation, and an important means of shaping the political culture of the society. Indoctrination was an effective form of political socialization which involved individuals in the political system.

---

[18] Daniel Bell, "The End of Ideology in the Soviet Union," in Milorad Drachkovitch, editor, *Marxist Ideology in the Contemporary World: Its Appeals and Paradoxes* (Stanford, Calif.: Hoover Institution Press, 1966), p. 107.

[19] Compare the views of Joseph M. Bochenski and Daniel Bell, in Drachkovitch, editor, *Marxist Ideology in the Contemporary World*, op. cit., pp. 60-120.

Ideological manipulation, once its efficacy was discovered, was continually exploited to invade totally the minds of the people. State-controlled press, literature, and broadcasting were transformed into one huge "machinery of the lie." The system of political education enveloped all groups in society. Special political schools, universities of Marxism-Leninism, study circles in the armed forces, and special committees of political enlightenment in factories and in "houses of culture" were bound to create a "new communist individual" completely subservient to the party.[20] Yet despite all these precautions, it did not prove true that "lies continuously repeated sound like truth." The common sense of the public has never been totally destroyed by party indoctrination. True, some people began to accept ideology without question. The drumbeat repetition of the same ideological lessons "totally stripped them of critical thought."[21] Others, however, ceased to react at all to ideological stimuli. The effectiveness of ideological manipulation has diminished considerably in the last 40 years. The repeated Soviet "counterrevolutions" and "periods of deviations," the successive disclosures of fallacies of the regime, gradually destroyed the "magic" of Marxism-Leninism.

This growing ideological crisis was most strongly felt in the middle ranks of society in the Soviet bloc countries. The top party layers (which comprise the relatively small ruling elite, subservient apparatchiks, and occupants of the main *nomenklatura* positions) obviously take advantage of ideological manipulation, and it would be naive to believe they would give it up of their own free will. On the other hand, the relatively small group of dissenters at the "bottom" of the social structure had never believed in Marxism-Leninism, but had always pointed to the "glaring defects" of communism and had tried to show how it was refuted by "the growing body of scientific knowledge." The most important symptom of the ideological crisis came, therefore, when Marxism-Leninism began to lose its influence on the intermediate social strata.

This "center" of the social structure of a communist society comprises three important groups. The first—consisting of those who have participated in "internal emigration"—includes those who are almost totally indifferent to political issues, neither believing in ideological clichés nor willing to fight against them. They do not accept the regime; their main concern is merely "to be left alone." The second group of "passive observers" brings together skeptics and opportunists who do not refuse participation in the regime but try to minimize it. Though not believing in the communist ideology, they are ready to follow cynically those who offer the biggest

---

[20] See Robert Conquest, *Politics of Ideas in the USSR* (London: The Bodley Head, 1967), pp. 97-117.

[21] Compare the examination of A. Zinoviev's points on this matter by Leszek Kolakowski, in Drachkovitch, editor, *East Central Europe*, op. cit., p. 44.

benefits, and to pay lip service to those ideological clichés which are most profitable at the moment. The third group—and the one which is most important for the communist leaders—consists of the "active participants" who really believe in the regime's ideological goals and are wholeheartedly engaged in the creation of "a Soviet World Republic." This group provides the party with members who are ready not only to make party careers, but also to fight for the future of communism. The continuous dwindling of this group, which in some of the communist-ruled countries has almost ceased to exist at all, is the most spectacular effect of the crisis of communist ideology.

So, if the essence of the ideological crisis lies in the gradual shrinking of the group of "true believers" in Marxism-Leninism, the question is raised: Does it make any sense to continue to protect ideology if almost nobody believes in its "historical mission," in its capability to indicate the direction of the system's future development? Is it still useful to defend the ideology whose mobilizing and unifying role has recently deteriorated and whose defects have become broadly known? The answer of the Soviet ruling elite is a definite "yes." Marxism-Leninism is still highly significant for the Soviet rulers. It has ceased to be the basis for the political judgments of this group, but it still provides an effective means of control, of ensuring the uniformity and mental subjugation of society. It still allows the ruling elite to "stigmatize" anyone it dislikes as an "enemy of the people" without an official trial.

In conclusion, it is clear that Solzhenitsyn's advice to the Soviet leaders to abandon Marxism-Leninism will not be followed. They will not give up an instrument that continues to be useful for political control. It is not ideology that binds their hands; it is the system of totalitarianism which has created the "vicious circle" of the Soviet regime. Some Western commentators were right in observing that, in a way, Marxism-Leninism is like a book which has lost its substance. Yet books also have jackets which are often eye-catching and attractive. Books need not be read; they may serve as a pleasing decoration.

The window-dressing character of Marxism-Leninism has had important social, moral, and economic repercussions, however, which were scarcely noticed at the time either by communist rulers or Western commentators. The fact that ideological criteria were losing credibility as the standard of social behavior inevitably led to the creation of a double standard of public morality. Under pressure from the regime, the public had to observe ideological tenets although they could not be forced to respect them. Books without substance, even though decorative, are not taken seriously.

Ideology served for a while to retard the process of moral corrosion in socialist societies. Communism itself is a sort of religion. The blind belief in Marxist-Leninist dogmas deprived the society of the capability to think independently; but ideology did serve, on the other hand, to provide a sort of "quasi-moral" dogma which reduced the pure cynicism of individual attitudes. As ideological values began to lose their authority, however, this resulted in a further drastic decline in public morality. The awareness of ideological decay corrupted a generation of party members. They came to understand that, in fact, coercion is useful not to protect ideological values but to protect their own privileges—privileges which are obtainable by simple loyalty to the party elite and which, in any other circumstances, would not be tolerated by society. The lack of ideological illusions helped create what Lenin had called "conventional hypocrisy." The devaluation of ideology has had an equally demoralizing effect on the rest of society. Workers began to realize that a double standard of morality means one morality for the party elite and another for nonparty people and even for ordinary party members. They realized that corruption had become institutionalized by the system—so much so that it had become the unofficial method of distributing goods which were seldom available on the open market.

This realization has seriously undermined the system of public property, the central characteristic of communism. The ordinary citizen argues that, if the state doctrine is only a facade, then public property—sanctified by the ideology—actually belongs to no one. Hence, the "seizure" of public property has nothing to do with theft. It is prohibited by law but legitimized by public morality. Or rather, to be more precise, there are two public moralities—official and private. If an act of "seizure" of public property is officially revealed, an individual will be publicly condemned; otherwise, even if the act is broadly known, it will not meet public ostracism but, in many instances, understanding and assistance. In the double standard of public morality, the rule of "live and let live" has become sacrosanct.

For decades party leaders believed that the state derived many benefits from this rule, which was commonly known and accepted by authorities. According to an unofficial party interpretation, it made sense to tolerate a moderate level of corruption. Among its advantages from the state's point of view was the fact that the public seemed more intimidated, more dependent on authorities, more controllable. Under such a system, those who steal can be condemned anytime. If public opinion accepts that everyone steals if he wants to live, it will accept the fact that everyone can be punished if the state so desires. The individual must live with the understanding that the state's tolerance can cease at any time.

Crimes against public property are revealed constantly and do not surprise anyone. If someone is to be removed from the political scene or is simply inconvenient for local party leaders, authorities do not have to seek evidence of political unorthodoxy. Too many political trials give the impression that society is not as unified as the party likes to pretend. While at times it is useful to make a show of examples of political treason to prove that a struggle with internal and external enemies continues and that the party remains vigilant, at other times it is more convenient to deny the existence of political turbulence altogether. Then common bribery can provide a pretext for punishing an inconvenient individual. It can be an excellent instrument of political blackmail.

This does not mean that the Communist Party consciously created the system of "double morality." It simply accepted it and tried to derive from it as many benefits as possible. With time, however, the advantages of such a strategy seemed less and less clear cut. The collapse of public morality contributed explicitly to all of the distresses of the Soviet economy discussed above: low labor discipline, neglect of equipment, absenteeism, bribery, unproductive work, total lack of interest in quality output, and so on. The society created new unofficial techniques of social compensation for the unfairness of communism, methods of competition for benefits available only in backstage struggles, means of circumventing the pretended social equality. The system created not only a black market and corruption, but also unofficial channels through which decisions of all kinds are made. A "double morality," in fact, is linked with the "double life" of the whole society.

What are the chances of moral recovery of the communist society? It has been noted that the top party leaders cannot be treated in common with the rest of the contestants who fight for their "share of no one's property." In their approach to consumer goods, they rather resemble the group of rulers from Plato's *Republic*. They seem to possess nothing but control everything. Their recent attempts to eliminate the system of "double morality" and to reconstruct the communist "collective mentality" seem to be genuinely motivated.

But their chances of reforming the system are slim. The apparently modest standard of living and relatively low salary of Brezhnev, Andropov, or Chernenko should not delude anyone.[22] The Polish crisis provided enough evidence that the party leadership is no less corrupt than the bottom of society. It is just that the highest ranks of the party elite are usually struggling for privileges that are beyond the reach or ambition of ordinary citizens. Their apparent "puritanism" stems simply from the fact that they are entitled to "open accounts" at the State Bank. At their level, not consumer goods but pure power is the main object of competition.

Even so, the unique position of the party elite has not entirely served to isolate them from the temptation of corruption and "unofficial" methods of distributing consumer goods. As Arnold Beichman and Mikhail S. Bernstam have pointed out.

---

[22] Brezhnev had a salary of probably no more than 100 rubles ($1,205) per month—less than he was earning as a Lieutenant General. See John Dornberg, *Brezhnev: The Mask of Power* (London: Andre Deutsch, 1974), p. 289.

The "second economy," or the "gray-black" economy, is what makes the Soviet state function. The "second-economy" is what makes life bearable for everybody. The consumer can obtain various kinds of foods, goods, and services otherwise unobtainable in official shops. The people who provide these foods, goods, and services profit and can in turn better their life through the "second economy." The "second economy" system is what provides the incentives for people to produce. To weaken these incentives by a drive against "corruption" will decrease what productivity exists now.[23]

Lower-level party leaders watch carefully for every possibility to grasp privileges which they still do not possess. Backstage mechanisms, corruptive techniques, unofficial strategies—all are part of their repertoire. Thanks to the lack of democratic control, such techniques are inherent to the Bolshevik system of power, which protects all its fossilized components. The Soviet "vicious circle" is closed around the sphere of public morality.

The "Dictatorship of Ignoramuses"

A question which is often put to emigrés and defectors from Eastern bloc countries concerns the competence of those in *nomenklatura* positions who occupy hundreds of thousands of main posts in science, education, agriculture, and industry.[24] Is it really true that their ineptitude results in incalculable losses for the communist economy? Are they really so incompetent and their decisions so foolish?

Responding to such inquiries, Soviet propagandists and Western radicals usually point out that the level of education in socialist countries is superior to that in the West. The West should worry, they say, that in the future "Johnny will not read" while "Ivan will read, and read fluently." Moreover, the advances of science and technology in Soviet institutes, laboratories, and universities produce specialists who are at least equal to those in the West. Such statements are for the most part correct. The Western system of education leaves much to be desired. Additionally, science, technology, and even "properly directed" research in the humanities have received broad and solid support from communist governments, and have produced a considerable body of scholarly and scientific findings. Yet all of this does not change the fact that Soviet decisionmakers are thoroughly incompetent and that incompetence is implicit in the recruiting system for the communist *nomenklatura*. Before we delve deeper into this problem, some explanation of the transformation which the system of party bureaucracy has undergone in the post-Stalinist period will be required.

---

[23] Beichman and Bernstam, *Andropov*, op. cit., p. 202.

[24] The system of *nomenklatura* was established during 1946 and 1947, and it consisted originally of about 40,000 newly promoted officials and newly approved old apparatchiks. In the 1950s, this network was substantially extended. See ibid., p. 103.

The death of Stalin began a new era for the regime. It was obvious that the system created by Stalin had been consolidated and that the absence of its creator did not jeopardize its basic tenets. The crucial principle of one-party rule, which in fact meant the power of a small elite headed by a single leader, was left untouched.[25] Yet the system required some modification. In Stalin's time, even the top-ranking members of the party elite felt extremely insecure. This inevitably reduced the appeal of a party career. The younger generation of party leaders was much more pragmatic, much less dedicated to revolutionary ideas. They wanted to enjoy their "share in power" without the risks that had accompanied their predecessors' endeavors.

At the same time, the system of "supplementation" of the acting party elite required some improvement. Khrushchev's generation understood perfectly Vilfredo Pareto's theory of the "circulation of elites." The rule of the party elite, "the guiding force of the proletariat," was taken for granted. It was obvious that elites ruled in all societies. Yet their success depended upon their degree of flexibility. Only "open" elites, which were ready to co-opt the most flexible social elements, were able to survive. Based on this premise, the Communist Party concluded that it had to involve more groups in its politics by giving them the impression that they might be able to participate in the decisionmaking process. The only qualification for co-optation into the higher ranks was to be acceptance of the politics of those presently running the party and skill in presenting ideological clichés.

In looking for new recruits, the party leaders obviously sought people from whom both loyalty and expertise could be expected. Not surprisingly, the combination of both characteristics in the same person was hard to find. In fact, a system based on arbitrary decisions frequently changed by the party leaders could not really welcome experts. On the contrary, professional skills and values were incompatible with the principle of *partiinost*, which declared that the party was always correct. The system led to the method of "negative selection," which promoted only compliant, comfortable "yes-men." Individuals who combined this adaptable trait with a particular ruth-lessness had the best prospects for a party career. In fact, *nomenklatura* did not require traditional education, but rather "talents" of a special type. Party officers and managers were not selected on the basis of professional or even bureaucratic ability. Professionals who could think independently and crit-icize openly were disqualified as candidates for *nomenklatura* positions. To the party elite, reliability was far more important.

---

[25] The dogma has not changed since Lenin's time. In his address on the Lenin Anniversary, in 1982, Yuri Andropov once more expressed the party's condemnation of political pluralism. Where there is "no private ownership of the means of production," Andropov said, "there is no place for the promotion of political parties hostile to socialism." Cited by Ebon, *The Andropov File*, op. cit., p. 92. For a broader discussion of succession and turnover of Soviet elites, see Seweryn Bialer, *Stalin's Successors* (Cambridge: Cambridge University Press, 1980), pp. 63-126.

To perform routine activities throughout the country, the regime had to replace Stalinist terror with a more effective system of rewards and incentives. As a result, unaccountability and tolerance of irresponsibility, incompetence, and corruption became the price paid in exchange for the loyalty of the *nomenklatura* to the party elite. As long as a person on the list did not act against the party elite, he usually could expect to remain in one *nomenklatura* position or another, regardless of his fitness for the job. Anyone who demonstrated extreme stupidity or incompetence was simply transferred to another post, thereby accounting for the impression that, in exchange for his loyalty, he would gain security and the protection of the system.

The party elite consisted of persons who, though they competed among themselves, were capable of mutually supporting one another against elements from outside the party system which could jeopardize their careers. Thanks to these arrangements, the system was relatively fluid and able to survive the long period of totalitarian rule. The multitudinous *nomenklatura* allowed the Communist Party to involve a sizable group of adaptable people in its affairs. To be on the *nomenklatura* list meant having a better paying job, a better apartment and a car, better and quicker prospects for promotion to a higher bureaucratic office, a feeling of protection and immunity, and participation in the decisionmaking process. In return, one had only to follow the Communist Party line. To oppose this line meant being deprived of everything; it meant having one's career ended instantly. Even professionals with graduate degrees found it difficult to return to normal work. It was not easy for a bureaucrat of 10 or 20 years standing to begin a new career as a engineer or physician having been deprived of all the accustomed benefits. Being crossed off the *nomenklatura* list meant having to depend on people who had previously been subordinates. In most cases, someone who had been removed from the list felt alienated from the socialist elite and deprived of all prestige and social acceptance. This serious psychological pressure enabled the party to manipulate *nomenklatura* without restraint.

It is, therefore, senseless to ask whether such and such a top-level party leader or even the rank-and-file apparatchik is more or less "civilized" or educated. When the utter lack of moral scruples is a condition for elevation to the top ranks, it is foolish to expect those who have made it to the top suddenly to display traits that would disqualify them for their positions of power. The fact is that those who are innocent, competent, principled, insufficiently malleable, or lacking in ruthlessness have no chance whatsoever of reaching the top.

The successful climb to the top of the party pyramid instills in the mind of an apparatchik or party technocrat the conviction that ruling others is his own personal right. He begins to treat a communist enterprise, factory, educational center, or hospital as his own possession. A member of the *nomenklatura* experiences an emperor-like power in his or her territory. He begins to reward friends and relatives, punish enemies, and modify decisions in return for bribes. The process of "climbing" to the top seems itself to legitimize his conduct.

In the Brezhnev era some steps were taken to improve the system of selecting members of the party cadres.

Great emphasis has been placed in recent years both on upgrading the leadership skills of party cadres through extensive reeducation programs and on the mastery of sophisticated managerial techniques borrowed almost wholly from the West. In pragmatic terms "competence" has become the watchword in the evolution of party and state cadres. While other, more traditional aspects of leadership, such as a sense of partiinost (partyness), must also characterize the model executive, Brezhnev made it clear in his comments to the Twenty-Fifth Congress that the themes of "thorough competence, discipline, and an initiative-taking, creative approach" to management were now clearly the operative standards.[26]

Andropov, in his first major address, made the same pronouncements. But Martin Ebon, author of a biography of Andropov, was able to show that Andropov's sharp criticism of the communist bloc's managerial deficiencies was almost identical to remarks offered by G.M. Malenkov 30 years before.[27] It did not surprise anybody that, shortly after his elevation to the position of General Secretary, Mikhail Gorbachev proclaimed a new period of constructive reforms in the Soviet Union.

Each successive generation of Soviet leaders brings new declarations, and each bequeaths more dissatisfaction to the Soviet public. In his excellent study, *The Modernization of Soviet Industrial Management*, William J. Conyngham writes about the last period of Brezhnev's reformative efforts in the Soviet Union:

. . . as Soviet management enters a new decade, it seems evident that the modernization of industrial management has reached an impasse. Further organizational development requires relatively fundamental structural change. The patterns of institutional change over the past fifteen years suggest, however, that such a far-reaching adaptation of industrial organization is highly unlikely to come about under Brezhnev's political leadership.[28]

---

[26] Donald R. Kelley, "The Communist Party," in Kelley, editor, *Soviet Politics in the Brezhnev Era*, op. cit., pp. 33-34. The process of professionalization within the Soviet *nomenklatura* and even within the Soviet administration seems to be overestimated in the West. In my opinion, the system of recruitment to *nomenklatura* is permanently crippled, and leads to a lack of real managerial experience and a lack of incentives for effective management. Professional qualifications and education cannot cure the whole system. See also Bialer, *Stalin's Successors*, op. cit., pp. 165-177.

[27] Ebon, *The Andropov File*, op. cit., pp. 128-129.

[28] William J. Conyngham, *The Modernization of Soviet Industrial Management* (London: Cambridge University Press, 1982), p. 272.

It does not seem to be any more likely under Brezhnev's successors. In a closed society which does not tolerate open criticism, professionals will always pose a threat to the secure position of the leaders. Incompetent party leaders not only personally interfere in detailed economic problems, but apparently even feel an obligation to do so. Every step in their political career teaches them that the party is infallible, and that they share infallibility of a sort with the entire organization. The party and its vanguard cannot err. This system does not need and cannot endure experts who could reveal the mistakes of the ruling elite. Mistakes are not possible because "a defeat" is something alien to communism. That reasoning closes this "vicious circle": If the party and its leaders cannot be wrong, then every economic failure of the acting leadership must be presented as a victory. The Chernobyl tragedy provides one of the numerous examples of this phenomenon. The clear failure of the Soviet leaders to control the disaster and inform neighboring countries was covered up by heroic stories and Gorbachev's statement that the Party successfully handled the situation from the very beginning.

Except during periods of succession crisis, when predecessors can be criticized, the leadership shows a total inability to break out of this economic and political deadlock. The "Dictatorship of Ignoramuses" (as it was called by Stefan Kisielewski) is a permanent component of the Soviet system.

What Handicaps the Decisionmaking Process?

Every student of bureaucratic structures knows that no decisionmaking process can prove effective without at least several basic elements: competence, information, coordination, responsibility of policymakers, control over the implementation of decisions, and capability to learn from mistakes. In the preceding examination, the first item on this brief list was found sadly lacking. It must be said, however, that the Soviet system is equally deficient in the rest of the necessary elements.

A study of how policy choices are made in the Soviet-bloc countries finds that central planning, the policymaking process, and the implementation of crucial decisions are profoundly affected by the permanent lack of proper information. All bureaucratic organizations are built to act on rational premises. It is true that decisionmaking always involves some nonrational components when decisions take place under uncertainty and when the consequences of the choices are unknown. But the problem that handicaps the socialist economy is not simply the presence of nonrational factors in the decisionmaking process, but rather the overwhelming degree to which such nonrational determinants contribute to the final decision. Because of the predominance of nonrational factors, important choices are made without proper calculation, and wild predictions take the place of rational cost-benefit analyses. In the socialist system, which not only lacks proper information but is actually based on misinformation, the odds of increasing the role of rational factors in planning and decisionmaking are quite small. Without proper information, socialist decisionmaking processes will never fit the rational model.

Why is adequate information usually unavailable to Soviet economic management? It has often been emphasized by Western analysts that misinformation and disinformation play an important role in Soviet foreign policy and that propaganda and censorship help to manipulate political attitudes in Soviet bloc countries.[29] To exist, the system has to be protected from real information. Only selected information without alternatives can be approved. Information shapes the political culture of society; thus, communist leaders cannot afford to relinquish control over the dissemination of information, which serves as a convenient instrument of power.

This approach to the role of information stems from basic Leninist principles and cannot be properly grasped without an analysis of Lenin's concept of proletarian dictatorship. The problem was lucidly expressed by him in 1902 when he acknowledged that the Russian working class had proved itself incapable of exercising its own dictatorship. In his pamphlet, *What Is To Be Done?*, he clearly laid out his belief that the "history of all countries shows that the working class, exclusively by its own effort, is able to develop only trade-union consciousness, i.e., the conviction that it is necessary to combine in unions, fight the employers, and strive to compel the government to pass necessary labor legislation, etc."[30] There cannot be any independent ideology formulated by the working class itself. The spontaneous nature of things leads to the subordination of workers to the bourgeois ideology.[31]

---

[29] See Richard H. Shultz, Jr., and Roy Godson, *Dezinformatsia: Active Measures in Soviet Strategy* (Washington, D.C.: Pergamon-Brassey's, 1984).

[30] Vladimir I. Lenin, *Collected Works* (Moscow: Progress Publishers, 1964), Vol. V, p. 375. As Richard Pipes proved convincingly, at this time Lenin was strongly influenced by his awareness that the labor movement in Russia and the political movement of Social Democratic intellectuals were developing independently. Richard Pipes, *Social Democracy and the St. Petersburg Labor Movement 1885-1897* (Cambridge, Mass.: Harvard University Press, 1963).

[31] Lenin, *Collected Works*, op. cit., Vol. V, pp. 284, 286, 442. Marx really seemed to have been turned on his head. It appeared that the socialist consciousness of the proletariat could be reached only in particularly favorable circumstances and after the intellectuals had explained to the workers what "socialism" really meant. A lot of questions were raised immediately: Does it mean that, if this socialist consciousness is not brought to the workers "from outside," socialism, so inevitable in Marx's concept, might not come into existence? Is this socialist phase of the dialectic development not spontaneously and necessarily imminent, but instead dependent upon the efforts of a few activists and theoreticians? What will happen if the revolutionary intellectuals differ in their concept of socialism? Which group should be followed by the proletariat? Whatever can be said about the flexibility of Lenin's arguments, these questions can hardly be answered satisfactorily solely by reference to Marxist theory. All of them were often raised by Western critics, and were always perplexing for the Russian orthodoxy. See Merle Fainsod, "Bolshevism Before 1917," in Samuel Hendel, editor, *The Soviet Crucible: The Soviet System in Theory and Practice* (Duxbury, Mass.: Duxbury Press, 1980), pp. 44-45; Daniel Bell, "Two Roads from Marx," in *The End of Ideology* (Glencoe, Ill.: Free Press, 1960), pp. 354-355; Daniel Bell, *Marxian Socialism in the United States* (Princeton, N.J.: Princeton University

Undoubtedly this was the most basic theoretical step taken by Lenin toward totalitarianism. His reasoning was clear. The revolution was an ultimate goal, and it could be accomplished by the proletarian dictatorship without waiting for the mature economic conditions believed necessary by Marx. Yet this whole concept made no sense if the existing proletariat was incapable of seizing dictatorial power. Lenin had to find some means that would enable the proletariat to assume the reins of government despite its immaturity. He believed that his vision of the Communist Party could provide the proper solution. The party had to represent "all." It had the exclusive right to educate workers. Anyone who was not with the party was against it. The revolution and the future of communism were identified with the party.[32]

The totalitarian consequences of this basic assumption are quite visible. According to Lenin, the immature working class can be manipulated by anybody. To prevent this, it should be "educated" by the Communist Party. Workers should be "educated" even if this education is totally incompatible with their wishes and aspirations. The Communist Party always knows what constitutes "correct" wishes. This is not "manipulation"; it is "training."[33] The party, said Lenin, could speak for the whole working class. Once properly educated, the workers would follow the party line in the future.

The idea that "the party is always right" was the first meaningful totalitarian conclusion to stem directly from Lenin's theory of the party. The next was the conviction that only one organization could legitimately represent workers: "our" party. "We" always meant "the strongest," "the most dedicated," "the most ruthless"—simply those who, irrespective of means, won the workers' trust in the decisive moment. Until his death, Lenin seemed sincerely to believe that only he (and his Bolshevik Party) could speak for the Russian proletariat. The working class was one body and it could be represented only by a single party. Individuals and their wishes were meaningless, as it was the party that always knew what was best for them. As Leonard Schapiro has written, "The individual would no longer require

---

Press, 1967), pp. 14-15; David Lane, *Politics and Society in the USSR* (New York: New York University Press, 1978, 2nd edition), pp. 13-14.

[32] Lenin expressed it fully before the Tenth Congress of the Party in 1921: "Marxism teaches—and this tenet has not only been confirmed in practice by our revolution—that only the political party of the working class, i.e., the Communist Party, is capable of uniting, training and organizing a vanguard of the proletariat and of the whole mass of the working people that alone will be capable of withstanding the inevitable petty-bourgeois vacillations of this mass and the inevitable traditions and relapses of narrow craft unionism or craft prejudices among the proletariat, and of guiding all the united activities of the whole of the proletariat, i.e., of leading it politically, and through it, the whole mass of the assumption are quite visible." Lenin, *Collected Works*, op. cit., Vol. XXXII, p. 246.

[33] As Leon Trotsky wrote, "the masses go into a revolution not with a prepared plan of social reconstruction, but with a sharp feeling that they cannot endure the old regime. Only the guiding layers of a class have a political program." Leon Trotsky, *The Russian Revolution* (New York: Doubleday, Anchor Books, 1959), p. x.

any means of protection against his 'own' party and his 'own' state."[34] Lenin rejected the concepts of pluralism, diversity of interests and opinions, spontaneous economic rules, and individual freedom—all those factors that could limit the totalitarian propensities of the state.

Lenin was aware that the revolution could survive only by rejecting democratic institutions, but that it nevertheless had to pay lip service to democratic clichés. The party therefore had to learn methods of manipulation—of presenting to the world a facade of apparently democratic institutions. In accordance with party "jargon," the leaders had to learn how to follow Lenin's art of "deduction of the mood of the masses."[35] Lenin understood that the masses would follow those who were most persuasive, those most capable of proving that they could "correctly" read the will of the people.

The concept of exclusive power in one party had far-reaching consequences. It helped to solidify the dogma that the communist party, as a whole, was always right.[36] Even innocent individuals could be sacrificed for the party because it exclusively represented the ultimate "rightness." The dogma that the fate of the party should be identified with the fate of the revolution was, with time, transformed into the official policy that the future of the party and the future of communism were simply the same.

From the assumption that the party as such could never be wrong, it also followed that Marxism-Leninism, recognized as an official and exclusive ideology, could be interpreted only by the party. In this process, any dogma once presented and accepted as part of the party's creed could never be revised. Party decisions might be rectified, but they could not be admitted as mistakes. Moreover, one had to restrict oneself to the discussion and exposition of only those communist truths which were supportive at that point of the party's policies. Other dogmas, inappropriate or embarrassing for the moment, did not have to be renounced or shed but rather should be discreetly held in limbo to be called up when the time was ripe for their use. The truth was not judged on its own merits, but according to a typically communist pragmatic principle known as *partiinost*. "Correct" or "right" was anything considered to be such by the party, anything "that the party at any time commanded, and, most important at the time when the party commanded."[37]

---

[34] Leonard Schapiro, "Lenin After Fifty Years," in Leonard Schapiro and Peter Reddaway, editors, *Lenin, The Man, The Theoretist, The Leader: A Reappraisal* (New York: Frederick A. Praeger, 1967), p. 11.

[35] Trotsky, *The Russian Revolution*, op. cit., p. 114.

[36] See Trotsky, quoted by Borris Souvarine, *Stalin* (New York: Longmans, Green, 1938), pp. 362-363.

[37] See A.P. Ohloblyn's lecture on Soviet historiography, given at the Symposium of Refugee Scholars and Scientists Who Have Escaped From the USSR, *Academic Freedom Under the Soviet Regime*, New York, April 3-4, 1954.

This approach was not new. Lenin explained the foundations of the principle of *partiinost* in his pamphlet, *Party Organization and Party Literature*, published in 1905. He wrote:

What is this principle of party literature? It is not simply that, for the socialist proletariat, literature cannot be a means of enriching individuals or groups: it cannot, in fact, be an individual undertaking, independent of the common cause of the proletariat. Down with non-partisan writers! Down with literary supermen! Literature must become part of the common cause of the proletariat, "a cog and a screw" of one single great Social-Democratic mechanism set in motion by the entire politically conscious vanguard of the entire working class. Literature must become a component of organized and integrated Social-Democratic Party work.[38]

In 1917, Lenin was completely convinced that the revolutionary events had proved him right. Everybody who was not with him was against the party and the revolution. In his work there was no room for neutrality or objectivity. Information was good when it was "correct," i.e., useful for the party. The revolutionary struggle, he used to repeat, proved that "when every minute counts, when dissent and neutrality allow the enemy to put in his word, when he will certainly be heard, and when no haste is made to help the people in their struggle for their sacred rights, I cannot call such a stand neutrality; a revolutionary would call it indictment."[39] The problem was that, for his successors, the revolutionary struggle was endless, the state of emergency lasted forever, and only their voice was always "correct," while the dissents of others were nothing more than baldfaced attempts to deceive the people. The exclusive right of the party leadership to interpret communist tenets left plenty of room for the manipulation of all kinds of information.

The differences between the mentalities of Lenin and Stalin caused the latter, who lacked Lenin's fanatical character, to go a step beyond his mentor. Lenin decided to give power to the party elite; Stalin did not see any difference between a small group and one person being in power. Stalin inherited from Lenin a deep disbelief in the popularity of socialism, but Lenin wanted to believe that the "weakness" of the proletariat would be of a temporary character; Stalin had an essentially pessimistic approach to the masses. He had many more doubts than Lenin that the working class would ever be capable of accepting the communists without coercion.[40] In fact, Lenin attempted, like Stalin, to impose his will upon the whole party. But at least he also tried to convince his associates that he was right. Stalin,

---

[38] Lenin, *Collected Works*, op. cit., Vol. X, p. 45. It is worthwhile to compare Lenin's and Marx's views on the free press: see Lenin, "How to guarantee the success of the Constituent Assembly," *Collected Works*, op. cit., Vol. XXV, p. 375; Karl Marx, *Collected Works*, Vol. I (London: Lawrence & Wishart, 1975), pp. 132-181, 349.

[39] Lenin, *Collected Works*, op. cit., Vol. 26, pp. 229-230.

[40] Isaac Deutscher, *Stalin: A Political Biography* (London: Oxford University Press, 1949), p. 262.

lacking the authority of his predecessor, simply exterminated all who were at odds with him. Lenin believed that his party was always right. Stalin believed that he had a right, made sacred by his revolutionary career, to speak in the name of the party. It was Lenin's rule that the interest of the revolution justifies everything. In Stalin's time, Lazar Kaganovitch openly transformed this thesis into a slogan that the party's interest is utmost. Stalin expressed this dogma in more Machiavellian form: "For the good of the party, every method is permissible."[41] In Lenin's time, the control of society was a means without which the party could not survive. In Stalin's period, it became the end in itself. Terror, used only occasionally in Lenin's time, became the most conspicuous political tool of Stalin's reign.

Lenin believed that the immature proletariat could not be properly informed about the decisions of the party elite. Stalin went a step further: he started to create myths. In the Stalinist era misinformation became an essential element of Sovietization. Stalin's successors have introduced some cosmetic changes in the totalitarian structures of the Soviet system, but they have never dared to depart from Stalin's and Lenin's approach to the problem of information. The shock engendered by Nikita Khrushchev's denunciation of the crimes of the Stalin era was a telltale indication of what was to come. Soviet leaders have never been able to overcome their fear that a free flow of information would open a "Pandora's box" of public hatred accumulated over many years. The events in Hungary and Czechoslovakia and the successive Polish upheavals seem to confirm their fears.

All these phenomena were from time to time identified by Western analysts, but their consequences were seldom submitted to deeper investigation. While misinformation was seen as the means of subjugating society and manipulating public attitudes, it was presumed that the party elite, which had at its disposal a widespread system of police control, was itself perfectly informed about the true state of things. The numerous party cadres subordinated to top party leaders were supposed to help maintain military control over the country, monopoly control of all means of communication and education, and complete state control over the economy, and were responsible for providing perfect information to their superiors. This is a complete misunderstanding of the real situation in socialist countries. The system which successfully keeps individuals totally obedient and almost completely deprived of all forms of privacy is entirely lacking any effective means of providing economic information or control.

In fact, the large number of overlapping intermediary organizations badly hampers the decisionmaking process. The functionaries of all ranks are

---

[41] On the position of Kaganovitch, see Conquest, *The Great Terror*, op. cit., p. 15. Stalin's phrase was placed under his official portraits. See Jack Fishman and Bernard B. Hutton, *The Private Life of Josif Stalin* (London: W.H. Allen, 1962), Stalin's portrait between pp. 96 and 107.

equally interested in "success" and ready to misinform the central authorities. The hierarchical pyramid of control simply does not work. If the party cannot be wrong, then "success" must accompany all communist economic endeavors. This accounts for the fact that the party is totally incapable of learning from its mistakes. The constant push for economic success leads to the "overfulfillment" of all plans and the inclination to "maximize" output without regard for quality. It leads managers who are rewarded only for "successes" to conceal the real inefficiency of their enterprises. In a system in which production of predetermined quantities is the essential indicator of success, there are weak incentives to strive for more efficient production or reduction of expenditures.

Misinformation is implicit in the organizational inadequacies of the communist system. Some managers fake the accounts, others artificially exaggerate the quantity of production. In Polish coal mines, Solidarity revealed the existence of special machines that were imported to mix rock and soil with coal to double the apparent output. What is more paradoxical, the central authorities prefer not to be too well-informed. A friend of mine working on statistics at the police criminal office once explained to me how reports on criminal activity are put together. His task was to "improve" the data received from each police station to show a lower level of crime. "The Ministry of Internal Affairs," he explained, "would then review the composite report and most probably send it back for 'proofreading'—an euphemism for a downward revision of the figures. It is the routine procedure, repeated in each reporting period, regardless of the originally quoted figures." It is obvious that, in this situation, providing the correct information would certainly provoke denunciation. Higher party officials realize, however, that the *nomenklatura* members are, in fact, beyond accountability. Their job security is a reward for their reliability and their loyalty to the party elite. Their economic blunders are usually punished merely by transfer to another post. So long as they remain ideologically reliable, they are permitted to be equally incompetent in their new assignments. In this situation, information about their blunders is both ineffectual and politically inconvenient.

Inadequate information and deliberately distorted statistics handicap all economic planning and cripple all coordination. Harmonious functioning of the various economic sectors for more effective results cannot be properly established, if for no other reason than the shortages of materials, the production of which has been exaggerated in statistics. This causes supply dislocations and competition for resources among enterprises which, theoretically, should not exist in socialist industry.

Further contributing to the lack of accurate statistics and empirical data is the *partiinost* mentality of the Central Offices for Control of Press, Publication, and Performances. Their official Books of Directives and Recommendations set forth detailed instructions for the elimination of any negative comments on party decisions or any reference to official blunders or bungling. This obviously makes any serious discussion of economic fallacies impossible. Under so broad a censorship, basic economic, social, and political information goes unpublished. Costly scandals and blunders in urban planning, housing, and agriculture, and irrational decisions regarding investments, location, and production are withheld from the public. All scientific disciplines which rely on accurate statistics are hampered by such policies.[42] Reliance on similar misinformation, economic naivete unsupported by genuine economic research, and arbitrary decisions made by central authorities go a long way toward explaining the economic weakness of all communist countries.

In evaluating Soviet managerial behavior, one has to take into consideration the element of factionalism, another counterproductive component of the socialist economy. Contrary to Lenin's antipluralistic declarations, factionalism became the most notorious attribute of the socialist managerial structures. In fact, the deeper the fractionalization of socialist society, the stronger the tendency to declare its monolithic character. Stalin himself was the master of factional strategies. He repeatedly set up new factions and surrounded himself with the successive "inner circles" of party leaders. The members of these coteries were always threatened by the new coalitions formed by Stalin long before the existing factions could endanger his position. At the same time, Stalin succeeded in extracting himself from the restraining influence of factional politics, which helped him pretend that he alone sought to implement Lenin's concept of the monolithic party institution, which was apparently challenged by everyone but himself. As Carl A. Linden wrote, Stalin "curbed factionalism as an autonomous political factor within the Soviet and Moscow-led Communist parties. He became the final arbiter of all conflict, but he did not destroy the factional tendency."[43]

In the post-Stalinist era, factionalism was successfully employed by the middle and lower circles of the Soviet leadership, and factions became the vehicles through which economic, social, and political decisions were con-

---

[42] The official book of censorship reads like a historical novel. Here are a few examples from one of them: " . . . figures illustrating the state and growth of alcoholism on a national scale are not to appear in the mass media." "All information about the direct threat of industry and the use of chemicals in agriculture to human life and health must be expunged." "Information concerning Poland's purchase of licenses from capitalist countries is to be eliminated from the mass media." "All publications presenting general statistics with regard to conditions of safety and hygiene at work or to occupational diseases must be withheld." "Absolutely no information is to be published concerning the Katowice mine disaster in which four miners lost their lives." *Official Censorship in the Polish People's Republic* (Ann Arbor, Mich.: The North American Study Center for Polish Affairs, 1978), p. 4.

[43] Carl A. Linden, "Opposition and Factions in Communist Party Leadership," in Frank P. Belloni and Dennis C. Beller, editors, *Faction Politics: Political Parties and Factionalism in Comparative Perspective* (Santa Barbara, Calif.: Clio Books, 1978), p. 373.

veyed and important goals achieved.[44] Factions were to replace real intermediate social structures (religious groups, independent trade unions, spontaneous professional organizations) destroyed in the Stalinist era. Without them the party elite was losing contact with the grass-roots of society. The new generation of party executives at all levels of the party hierarchy began to set up new coteries based on reciprocal relations between patrons and clients. Patronage was the term used to explain the special complex of relations between those who used their influence and social position to assist and protect others who were ready to support blindly those who offered protection and assistance.[45] Clients helped patrons to succeed in their undertakings and reach the higher levels of the party hierarchy; once promoted, patrons were expected to elevate their clients as well. Mutual interest, which focused almost exclusively on the party career of both patrons and clients, was the best warrant of factional loyalty.

The system of patronage contributed to the process of creating the informal party framework which doubled the number of formal governmental structures. The existence of these two (governmental and party) pyramidal structures not only multiplied the red tape of the bureaucracy, but also introduced an element of uncertainty into its work. The party official who has to study carefully all patron-client relations is always exposed to the risk that, given their informal character, he can overlook some important ties in the system of patronage. It intimidates him, generates a lot of frustration, and, as a result, slows down the decisionmaking process and contributes to irregularities in his operations. Obviously, all these factors have a direct bearing on the implementation of decisions made under the system of central planning.

It was often argued that "even under ideal conditions the planning of the entire economy would probably involve a measure of inaccuracy because of statistical errors and unpredictable factors."[46] In the socialist economy, these inaccuracies were to be avoided by the perfect cooperation of all social groups. The collective mentality of the socialist society was to reduce to a minimum the unpredictable effects of central planning. As I have pointed out, the Marxist vision of a society that was united into a coherent whole never materialized. Actual fractionalization of the social structure magnified and continues to magnify the natural inaccuracies of the centrally directed economy.

---

[44] For a more detailed analysis of the process of the emerging of the new managerial elite in the post-Stalinist era see Jeremy R. Azrael, *Managerial Power and Soviet Politics* (Cambridge, Mass.: Harvard University Press, 1966), pp. 111-172.

[45] See Alex Weingrod, "Patrons, Patronage and Political Parties," in Steffen W. Schmidt, James C. Scott, Carl Lande, and Laura Guasti, editors, *Friends, Followers and Factions: A Reader in Political Clientism* (Berkeley, Calif.: University of California Press, 1977), p. 323.

[46] Joseph S. Berliner, *Factory and Manager in the USSR* (Cambridge, Mass.: Harvard University Press, 1957), p. 325.

27

It can be argued that the tendency to establish a patron-client relationship between persons of unequal status is typical not only of socialist societies. Vertical alliances which result in the fractionalization of social structures into a number of competing factional groups are visible to some extent in all types of social organizations. Factionalism is a phenomenon widely observed in the West. It is true that in free market economies factions are in a way a natural component of the competition which is the most vital element of the system. In contrast, in the centrally planned economy, which denies the stimulating impact of competition, factionalism is simply disastrous. It makes impossible coordination of planned economic projects and leads to increasing abandonment of cooperative activities which break down along the lines marking the factional divisions.

There is no evidence that factionalism among the socialist managerial cadres can be controlled or its harmful effects reduced. In fact, the career of the party leader can be promoted only through factions. The lack of genuine democratic mechanisms contributes to the fact that leaders emerge as a result of factional struggles. In a way, it is typical of all authoritarian and totalitarian systems. As Yi-Chun Chang wrote with regard to factional politics in China, "In a highly factionalized political setting, coalitions are the most practical, and, in fact, the only way to gain power and control."[47] Without introducing at least the rudiments of democracy, this method of leadership selection cannot be changed. On the other hand, the unadaptability of democratic mechanisms to the realities of the totalitarian system is the fundamental and unsolvable problem. Genuine democratic transformations would be disastrous for the system itself, and socialist leaders since Lenin's time have had a perfect understanding of this fact.

Each succession crisis brings some hope of recovery. Each new Soviet leadership admits some economic weaknesses and plans remedial actions, but the results are usually disappointing.[48] Despite repeated declarations of good intentions, it seems that up until now no adequate "model" for a true reform of the Soviet economy has been developed.

Reform proposals usually focus on a program of decentralization of the managerial system and emphasize the need for creating a system based on the profit motive, increasing efficiency and discipline in the workplace, giving greater responsibility to local managers, and so forth.[49] Each new

---

[47] Yi-Chun Chang, *Factional and Coalition Politics in China: The Cultural Revolution and Its Aftermath* (New York: Praeger, 1976), p. 127.

[48] See Robert Conquest, "Andropov and his Soviet Union," *Policy Review*, Summer 1983, p. 21.

[49] For more detailed analysis of the reform proposals, see Myron E. Sharpe, editor, *Planning, Profit and Incentives in the USSR*, Vols. I & II (New York: International Arts & Science Press, 1966). Especially instructive is the speech by A.N. Kosygin on "Improving Industrial Management, Perfecting Planning, and Enhancing Incentives in Industrial Production," published originally in *Izvestia*, September 28, 1965, Vol. II, pp. 3-46. For information on the most recent projects to improve economic performance in the Soviet Union, see Morris Bornstein, "Improving the Soviet Economic Mechanisms," *Soviet Studies*, January 1985, pp. 1-30.

party "team" has repeated that the decentralization of decisionmaking could trigger the real recovery of the communist system. Each has soon realized, however, that decentralization is incompatible with the political aspirations of the communist leadership. On the one hand, it is obvious that, given the lack of proper information at the top, local managers are better equipped to deal with economic reality. Hence, if economic efficiency is to be increased and delays in decisionmaking reduced, control of local management decisions by central agencies should be eliminated. On the other hand, short of returning to a system of market stimulants, the system of central control could be replaced only by the supervision of local workers' committees—a solution that could endanger party dominance. Economic power, once shifted to the working class, would lead to the growth of political power for the masses.

Communist theory assumes that political and economic resources of power are inseparable. The totalitarian system cannot be transformed into one that is merely authoritarian without posing a real threat to the ruling elite. Rank-and-file bureaucrats at the center are afraid of losing power, and their influence and even their jobs might be threatened. For this reason, attempts at decentralization have been uniformly superficial. In their final effect, such "reforms" have brought about only the further extension of bureaucracy and the creation of new intermediate bureaucratic structures which serve merely to convey the real decision made by functionaries at the center. Nor is this surprising, since both central and regional administrators want power, not responsibility. The center does not want to lose the appearance of economic control; the local agencies want to share power while bearing no responsibility for economic results.

The idea of "shared responsibility" between local and central agencies has failed miserably. In the Soviet system, the principle of "collective responsibility" is the first rule of social life and extends to the economic sphere as well. A collective is responsible for the correct behavior of its members, for the proper relationship between husband and wife, for the misbehavior of children, and so forth. In reality, this means that the collective can interfere in all aspects of social life, including the most intimate. This does not mean, however, that the collective is actually responsible for anything; "responsibility" is a term that everyone uses but no one takes very seriously. This approach has become an integral part of the socialist life-style. Barring fundamental changes in the system, therefore, it would be naive to expect that administrators will voluntarily accept more responsibility than absolutely necessary. People are not angels. It is difficult enough (and communists disregard this totally) for them to be human beings.

To recapitulate my analysis, I do not expect a recovery of the socialist economy for the following reasons:

(1) The system has forever destroyed the "collective mentality," which was to be a basic component of communist political culture.

(2) The crisis of communist ideology is irreversible. The belief of the masses in Marxism-Leninism cannot be reconstructed, yet socialist leaders will not give up obsolete dogmas because they do not know how to function without them.

(3) The ideological crisis has undermined the rudiments of communist morality and corroded all Marxist-Leninist values, including the key dogma of common ownership.

(4) The moral and ideological crisis has destroyed all healthy incentives among workers and managers.

(5) Without the nutriments of democracy people can be forced to work but they will not work efficiently. They will operate pursuant to the principle: "Those on the top pretend to share power with us, we pretend to work." Yet democratic transformations are too dangerous for the ruling elite. They are simply incompatible with the totalitarian framework of the system.

(6) The double standard of morality, together with massive economic dislocations, has created a black market and corruption, which have been tolerated for so long that they are now irrevocably integrated in the way of life in communist countries.

(7) The need for creating a relatively open party elite forced the party to build a system of "negative selection" that promotes compliant, conformable "yes-men" who care far more about their careers than about the system of communist values.

(8) Lack of competence, widespread corruption, and the unaccountability of decisionmakers are incompatible with the basic principles of economic efficiency.

(9) Lack of information, coordination, and proper control over the implementation of productive decisions, coupled with a form of decentralization that is more apparent than real, cripple the socialist system of central planning and decisionmaking.

(10) Without the party bureaucracy and the *nomenklatura* structure, the party cannot function; but with them, no reform is possible. Both are key ingredients of a system which can be overthrown but not reformed. They are an inseparable part of the system.

In 1982 some Western scholars referred to Andropov's plan of reform as "the task of Hercules in cleaning the Augean stables."[50] To the extent the "task" refers to real reform and not to a few superficial changes, the attempts of Andropov's successors will more nearly resemble the Sisyphean labors. The system itself has suppressed economic vitality and spontaneity, pro-

---

[50] Ebon, *The Andropov File*, op. cit., pp. 128-129.

tected its own incurability, and locked its leaders in the vicious circle created by their predecessors. So if I am asked about the chances for economic recovery of the Soviet system, my answer follows the old Roman formula: *Quod natura negat, reddere nemo potest.*

2.
Origins of the Crisis

THE ESSENCE of the "crisis" of communism, as we have seen, resides in two factors: (1) economic, moral, social, and ideological deformities of the Soviet system that are impervious to reform; and (2) the fact that widespread decay is steadily corroding the pillars of the communist totalitarian order. This second factor deserves more profound analysis.

It is not my intention here to define the nature of Soviet totalitarianism more precisely. That would require adding another volume to the numerous works already devoted to the same venture.[51] Instead, the remarks that follow will emphasize various aspects of totalitarianism which, for me, seem to be the most important and typical of the phenomenon. By summarizing the meaning of totalitarianism as it is used here, I hope to avoid any confusion that might arise from conflicting definitions.

Totalitarian dictatorship can be characterized by several main traits:

(1) The existence of an official ideology which sometimes causes leaders to act, but serves at other times to disguise the cynicism of the ruling elite and to rationalize actions that in fact are uncoordinated and ineffectual.

(2) Control by a single party, which is represented as a mass organization, but is in fact an elitist structure that co-opts into its top ranks individuals who are totally conformable to and compliant with the official party line. The party is usually headed by a very small group of activists, and often by a single autocrat who is presented as the charismatic leader of a nation, a class, or even the whole of mankind. The party is able to survive for a comparatively long time because its bottom ranks are relatively open and ready to accept anyone who blindly follows party orders.

(3) Operation of the party through a party bureaucracy and various intermediary associations completely devoted to the ruling elite. These numerous cadres, subordinate to top party leaders, help to maintain military control over the country, as well as monopoly control of all economic activity and of all means of communication and education.

---

[51] See the bibliography in Hannah Arendt, *The Origins of Totalitarianism* (New York: A Harvest/ HBJ Book, Harcourt, Brace, Jovanovich, 1973), pp. 483-507. Compare also the broader characterizations of totalitarianism: William Kornhauser, *The Politics of Mass Society* (Glencoe, Ill.: The Free Press, 1959); Carl J. Friedrich and Zbigniew K. Brzezinski, *Totalitarian Dictatorship and Autocracy* (Cambridge, Mass.: Transaction Books, 1980), pp. 2-9: Carl J. Friedrich, editor, *Totalitarianism* (New York: The Universal Library, Grosset & Dunlap, 1964); J. Lucien Radel, *Roots of Totalitarianism: The Ideological Sources of Fascism, National Socialism, and Communism* (New York: Crane, Russak & Company, 1975), pp. 13-36.

(4) The use of an extremely widespread system of police control, which helps to keep individuals totally obedient and almost completely deprived of all forms of personal life. The total domination of society by the state and the minimization of the private and individual sphere are not limited by law. Rather, the law serves only to enhance the power of the ruling elite. This total penetration of all spheres of social life by the state—including the ethical, religious, economic, and legal—distinguishes this system from all other dictatorships and autocratic regimes.

It is an illusion to assume that "the crisis" does not affect the key mechanisms of this totalitarian domination. In fact, the total subordination of the societies of the communist countries to the dictatorship of the party elites has always been based on a few techniques that have been interchangeably employed: the strategy of terror used most effectively by Stalin, the appealing promise of communist economic success used by Stalin's successors, and the ideological or nationalist euphoria which was exploited effectively during the post-revolutionary time and the period of war.

There is no question that communist regimes still exercise full internal control in the several Soviet-bloc countries. However, the strategies used to maintain this control are gradually being undermined by the crisis. More and more, the societies of the communist countries are aware that the alleged attractiveness of communism is illusory. Their belief in communist ideology is crumbling. Nationalist clichés do not appeal as strongly as before to people who want desperately to live on the level of civilized communities. Terror is still effective, but its excessively blatant application harms Soviet international relations, thereby threatening the system's long-term survival. For Soviet leaders, it is quite obvious that, without the cooperation and technology of the West, the economies of bloc countries will deteriorate further, just at a time when Western economies are on the mend. If these circumstances continue, Soviet participation in the arms race will place an unbearable strain on the economy. Mikhail Gorbachev's repeated calls for a renewal of the spirit of detente combined with his continuing sharp criticism of President Reagan's Strategic Defense Initiative program are the clearest indicators of the importance Kremlin leaders attach to the interrelationship among the domestic strategy of terror, successful participation in the armaments race, and undisturbed economic contacts with the West.[52] Mikhail Gorbachev is confronted with a crucial question that is undoubtedly provoking internal debate in the Soviet hierarchy: Whether to go on arming at the expense of the faltering economy, or to restructure a less restrictive social and economic system at the cost of nuclear and missile supremacy. He faces a serious dilemma: The reform and reconstruction process could

---

[52] See comments on Gorbachev's visit to France, "Gorbachev Calls for Detente," *Washington Post*, October 5, 1985.

lead to a real and dramatic recovery, but it could also imperil the totalitarian foundations of the state by relaxing its grip on Soviet life. Soviet leaders, on the other hand, might test an alternative strategy. They realize that renewal of a spirit of detente might extend the inflow of Western technology and capital to the Soviet bloc, and thus enable the Soviet Union to maintain strategic parity with the United States without suffering a further decline in the rate of growth of consumption and productivity.

The real reasons behind the Soviet interest in detente should be emphasized so that they are better recognized in the United States and Western Europe. The true Soviet motive has always been derived from a declining rate of growth in consumption and productivity. Yet, because of the shrewd manipulation of slogans, the issue of peace was offered as the real reason for the policy of detente. For almost two decades Soviet propaganda successfully exploited the Western mood, the Western aversion to war of any kind, and its concern for the welfare of its citizens. As a result of this policy, the Soviet Union (carefully concealing its own economic interest in detente) achieved at least strategic parity with the United States. The period of detente did not mean a reduction in military expenditures in the Soviet Union; on the contrary, there was a permanent expansion of Soviet nuclear and conventional armaments. As Seweryn Bialer wrote:

By far the most impressive achievement of the Brezhnev era and the greatest swing in Soviet capabilities has occurred in the military sphere. The Soviet Union achieved strategic parity with the United States; built up a numerical conventional preponderance in the European theater; increased immensely both its strategic and conventional strength in the Far Eastern theater; developed for the first time serious capabilities of global intervention, including the ability and the willingness to deploy large-scale surrogate interventionist forces far from its own borders; increased significantly the level of its military assistance in terms of arms sales, arms grants, and advisory personnel to friendly nations; and is engaged in yet marginally successful efforts to integrate more tightly the Warsaw Pact armed forces.[53]

Military power is still the principal instrument of Soviet policy aimed at the control of the satellite countries and extension of influence throughout the world. Soviet military expenditures, even taking into account the recent growth in U.S. defense spending during the first term of the Reagan Administration, still surpasses that of the United States. The report by the U.S. Secretary of Defense on Soviet military power in 1985 shows that

The cumulative cost of the Soviet military program during 1974-83 exceeds that of the United States by a large margin, despite a slowdown in the rate of overall

---

[53] Seweryn Bialer, "Soviet Foreign Policy: Sources, Receptions, Friends," in Seweryn Bialer, editor, *The Domestic Context of Soviet Foreign Policy* (Boulder, Colorado: Westview Press, 1981), pp. 411-412.

34

Soviet economic growth. During this decade, the estimated dollar cost of the total Soviet military program is 35 percent more than the comparably defined U.S. defense outlays, while the cost of Soviet weapons procurement is 50 percent greater . . . . Current estimates of Soviet military spending, in rubles from the early 1970s through the early 1980s, show a significant increase at a rate faster than overall economic growth. As a result, throughout the last decade, the Soviet military has absorbed an increasing share of the nation's estimated gross national product (GNP), a share now estimated at 15-17 percent. Even in a period of slowing economic growth, the Soviet military section continues to maintain its priority claim on the Soviet Union's economic resources.[54]

If the arms race continues, it is distinctly possible that the Soviet Union will not be able to keep pace with the more advanced American economy. The Soviet leaders realize that the dramatic recovery of the Soviet economy is impossible without restructuring the system or at least introducing some democratic or market concessions. A safer alternative for the Soviet bloc would be the transfer of technology and investment funds from the West. It is this route to economic growth that has spurred Gorbachev's campaign to promote the policies of nuclear freeze and detente. Detente might allow the Soviet Union to keep up militarily with the West without making dangerous domestic concessions or drastic reductions in the rate of growth of consumption. Military superiority over, or at least parity with, the West, combined with total control over the societies of the Soviet bloc, have always been the all-important targets of Soviet policy.

This strategy, however, might be undermined by the internal "crisis of communism." The crisis, even if not directly affecting the Soviet machinery of totalitarian control, might reduce chances for successful implementation of the detente policy. Repeated applications of terror and suppression, unaccompanied by efforts to attract the societies of the bloc countries by nationalistic, ideological, or economic stimulants, might result in the deterioration of relations with the West and consequently affect the Soviet military posture. Intervention in Afghanistan and the imposition of martial law in Poland prove that communist regimes continue to exercise control over rebellious people in their region. However, even the weak reactions of the West in these two instances sent the Kremlin leaders the signal that the repeated use of terror will severely affect West-East relations.

The paradox of communism is that, without totalitarian methods, the system can hardly survive, but with them, its rotten foundations cannot be restructured. Totalitarianism is a weapon that cuts both ways: it defends the ruling bureaucratic party elite but, on the other hand, undermines the pillars on which the power of this elite is based.

Totalitarian strategies and techniques were instrumental in enabling the Bolsheviks to subjugate the societies of Russia and the satellite countries of

---

[54] *Soviet Military Power 1985* (Washington, D.C.: U.S. Government Printing Office, 1985), p. 10.

Eastern Europe. It is often noted that, without its totalitarian methods of rule, the small Bolshevik Party would have vanished along with countless other revolutionary organizations. It would have lost its revolutionary identity by accepting numerous compromises. Without Lenin and his determination, the Soviet revolution simply would not have survived—at least not in the form favored by the Bolsheviks.

In short, the total dedication to one goal (revolution), the flexible interpretation of this goal to meet the momentary needs and desires of the Communist Party and its vanguard, and the readiness to use any and all means to accomplish the goal contributed to the final "success" of Bolshevism in Russia. Yet it remains a paradox that the greater the single-minded dedication to the revolutionary goal, the vaguer its meaning became. Everything that had been achieved was identified with "the goal." Communist flexibility has been shaped by a triumph of form over substance. The revolution that proved successful in Russia was not the same as the one anticipated by Marx; the Marxist facade had little in common with genuine Marxism. The "dictatorship of the proletariat" became the total subjugation of this class by a bureaucratic elite, while the principle of socialist democracy had as much to do with real democracy as national socialism had to do with socialism. This kind of "success" was little short of a defeat.

Bolshevism adopted the Machiavellian rule that "the end justifies the means." Yet the goal that was publicly proclaimed and the goal that was actually pursued were not the same. The result achieved could not justify anything, since it was itself unjust. The Bolsheviks found themselves in the role of a Faustus who paid the highest price for a lost youth which, when regained, seemed to provide few of the benefits of the vanished original. Yet the price had to be paid regardless of the customer's dissatisfaction. And this "price" is constantly being paid by the Russian communists. It is my thesis that total dedication to one purpose, together with a willingness to sacrifice all values that are precious to human beings in the name of this single purpose, have set in motion the process of the irreversible degeneration of the communist system. The creation of a gigantic empire with its potent military machine has been accomplished at the cost of economic collapse, ideological crisis, moral degeneration of the ruling elite, and social deviances affecting the entire society.

The main point of this study is that the "crisis" of communism is real and is corroding the framework of the communist totalitarian order. This corrosion can be observed, despite the fact that communist regimes still have total control over the situation in the Soviet bloc. The corrosion itself is not enough to undermine the regime so long as the Kremlin maintains its gigantic military machine. The crisis cannot be identified with the early collapse of the system, although it contributes to its current and future decay. What I precisely want to clarify is that more and more the communist

36

empire rests solely on one pillar, while the others are continuously being corroded and providing less and less support for the whole structure. This bare military power can for some time keep societies under control, but it is not enough to be the means of successful development. Societies deprived of moral strength and perspectives of economic and social progress cannot keep up with the more prosperous and free societies of the world. The moment of final "collapse" of the communist system cannot be precisely determined, but it seems quite certain that the gap dividing the West and the Soviet bloc will grow wider and wider. To understand the possible consequences of this situation, it is not only necessary to comprehend the meaning of the crisis, but also its origins and stages.

One of the questions most often put to me since I left Poland in 1982 is whether the crisis of communism will begin in that country. My answer is that it will not begin there, simply because it already began many years ago with the establishment of the first socialist state, the Soviet Union. The crisis began when Lenin implemented Marx's ideas in an underdeveloped country—the Russia of World War I. It unfolded during the periods of Stalin's purges, the revisionism of Khrushchev's era, Soviet interventions in Hungary, Czechoslovakia, and Afghanistan; and it most recently manifested itself in the Polish turbulence of the 1980s.

We will not attempt to examine all details of the development of the crisis. In my opinion, the crucial symptom signifying the corroding effects of the crisis is the growing awareness of the societies in the Soviet bloc that the crisis is real and its consequences are irreversible. The awareness of the crisis arises from the recognition of the complexity of factors which contribute to the economic, ideological, moral, and social fallacies of the system—from a consciousness of the permanent contradictions of the system. The awareness of the fact that the defects mentioned above are irremediable and reside in the inherent nature of the system itself multiplies the symptoms of the crisis, deprives the people of incentives to work, and reduces the number of activists and believers emotionally dedicated to communism. The awareness of the crisis is, in my opinion, its most important component. The process of awakening started with small intellectual centers and has gradually come to include one social group after another. It has occurred in all bloc countries, but in some of them (like Poland) it is more advanced than in others. There are several phases in this process and a logical sequence of events, which are worthy of attention.

The crisis began under Lenin and Stalin, but its stages were marked by the successive lessons learned by the societies of the Soviet bloc about the totalitarian nature of their system. The first stage to reveal the basic deficiencies of communism, which I call "the denunciation period," is linked to the relative relaxation of the post-Stalinist era. Czech, Hungarian, and Polish revisionism added a few new lessons to the knowledge of the basic strategies and tactics usually employed by totalitarian regimes. Revisionism at first examined and put to rest the myth that reform of the system could originate within the communist party; later, it dismissed as unrealistic the concept that changes initiated from outside the party would be deliberately and successfully continued by the regime's more progressive elements. The strategies of the organized anticommunist opposition, which pursued the utopian concepts of the spontaneous democratic and antitotalitarian transformation of the system, were tested primarily in Poland. Polish society was the first to reach the "mature consciousness"—recognition that the deviations of the system are basically irreversible and its totalitarian institutions can be crushed but not reformed. The establishment of Solidarity brought a temporary new tide of optimism, but it was quickly subdued by the decision outlawing the first independent trade union in the history of the communist system. Polish society was better prepared than other Soviet bloc societies to understand the nature of totalitarianism and more determined to defend itself against the consequences of the crisis. Yet the symptoms of the growing awareness of the crisis can also be observed to some extent in other countries. The Polish turbulence was only one link in the sequence of events whose logic can be understood only against the broader background of the "crisis of communism."

Marx argued that the communist revolution would require the "mature consciousness" of the proletariat, which would then better understand the contradictions and failings of the capitalist system. It is a paradox that the proletariat has finally acquired this consciousness not under capitalist rule but under *communist* rule, and that the phases of the proletariat's development mark at the same time major stages of the crisis of communism. This paradox is worthy of deeper consideration.

Lenin's Totalitarian Concessions

We have already examined the basic points of Lenin's reasoning which resulted in totalitarian consequences. The assumption that the inevitable revolution could begin in Russia, that it could be accomplished only through the dictatorship of the proletariat, and that the Russian proletariat was immature led Lenin to the conclusion that without the Communist Party the revolutionary task could not be implemented. His own party was obviously the best for this purpose. The problem was that, without revolutionary chaos, no communist party could anticipate certain success in any democratic election.

On the one hand, Lenin realized that the abdication of the Tsar and the victory of the Revolution gave a real advantage to the small but determined group of conspirators. Only they could transform the peculiarities of Russian political, social, and economic life from an obstacle into an opportunity. In the country that was "the weakest link of capitalism" the chances for seizure of power by a relatively small group of professional revolutionists seemed to be the greatest.

On the other hand, Lenin was aware that even after the February insurrection, the Bolsheviks remained a small and relatively unpopular minority among other revolutionary parties.[55] Even the overthrow of the Provisional Government and the seizure of power by the Bolsheviks did not give them a decisive majority in the electoral bodies—the Soviets and the Constituent Assembly. The Assembly, where the Bolsheviks gained only 25 percent of the vote (175 of the 707 seats), was promptly dissolved.[56] The Soviets (The Councils of the Workers' and Soldiers' Delegates), more sensitive to revolutionary rhetoric, survived. "All power to the Soviets" meant, however, controlled participation under the leadership of the party which took power by force.

These factors accounted for Lenin's belief that the revolution could be rescued only without democracy, and, if it was to be the Bolshevik revolution, he was absolutely right. Masters of the art of grasping power and of backstage manipulations, the Bolsheviks could not lead Russia along the parliamentary path. The party seized power and, as many Bolshevik leaders explicitly admitted, it could not relax its domination without the risk that it would be swept from power altogether.[57] Even if Lenin believed that in the future it would be possible to reconvert the dictatorship of the party into a dictatorship of the proletariat, actual practice proved that the party could never renounce its position without the risk of total defeat. The forced "education" of the masses appeared to be completely unsuccessful. In this sense, reality undoubtedly solidified Lenin's theoretical totalitarian construction.

The factor which influenced Lenin even more powerfully than the lack of full support in the elective bodies was the factional differences in his own party. Throughout his life Lenin argued with nearly everyone. The greater part of his articles consists of polemics and debates. He hardly trusted even his closest associates. "In the first days after his arrival" (April 1917), writes N. Sulhanov, "his complete isolation among all his conscious party comrades cannot be doubted in the least." "Even his party comrades, the Bolsheviks,"

---

[55] In his thesis (published in *Pravda* on April 7, 1917) on *The Task of the Proletariat in the Present Revolution*, Lenin insisted on "recognition of the fact that in most of the Soviets or Workers' Deputies our Party is a minority, so far a small minority, as against a bloc of all the petty-bourgeois opportunist elements, from the Popular Socialist and the Socialist-Revolutionaries down to the Organizing Committee (Chekheidze, Tseretele, etc.), Steklov, etc., etc., who have yielded to the influence of the bourgeoisie and spread that influence among the proletariat." Lenin, *Collected Works*, op. cit., Vol. XXIV, p. 22. See also J.P. Nettle, *The Soviet Achievement* (New York: Harcourt, Brace & World, 1967), p. 65.

[56] John Curtis, "The Russian Revolution of 1917," in Hendel, editor, *The Soviet Crucible*, op. cit., p. 84.

[57] See Isaac Deutscher, "Defeat in Victory," in ibid., pp. 92, 100.

confirms the Social Revolutionary Zenzinov, "at that time turned away in embarrassment from him." As Trotsky added, "the authors of these comments were meeting the leading Bolsheviks every day in the Executive Committee, and had first-hand evidence of what they said."[58] Lenin gained greater authority and personal prestige in May, but that did not change the fact that the oldest Bolsheviks, with Lev Kamenev and Gregory Zinoviev at the head, resisted his many proposals to the last, and especially objected to his theses on the immediate urgency of armed insurrection.

After the October Revolution, Zinoviev and Kamenev continued to oppose Lenin's policy, in a vain attempt to confine his radicalism. In November, they resigned again from the Central Committee, taking several other members of the party with them. Lenin answered once more with his *Letter to Comrades Kamenev, Zinoviev, Ryazanov and Larin*, demanding their complete subordination to the Central Committee.[59] At the time of the discussion of the Treaty of Brest-Litovsk, the opposition against Lenin was so strong that he offered his resignation twice. In June and August of 1918, a few senior Bolsheviks were assassinated in Petrograd and Moscow, and Lenin himself was seriously wounded by a Social Revolutionary, Fanya Kaplan.[60] All these events gave rise not only to the Red Terror (which began with the murder of the Tsar's family), but also provided arguments for Lenin's theoretical demand for the total control of the Bolshevik Party by its leadership and the crushing of opposition outside the party. If the Bolshevik revolution was to survive, the party vanguard led by Lenin was obliged to maintain its dictatorship. Only Lenin, as the Bolsheviks claimed, correctly anticipated the revolution. Only he and the group of his supporters, fanatically dedicated to the revolution, had the right to speak for all, to identify their decisions with the fate of the revolution. The concept of exclusive power in one party—the basic totalitarian tenet which originated in Lenin's theoretical assumption—seemed to be fully justified by the revolutionary realities. Once accepted, it had far-reaching consequences.

In addition, the new Bolshevik government was confronted with an extremely difficult economic situation. The chaos which had helped the Bolsheviks to grasp power began to jeopardize the revolution. The colossal economic collapse, which occurred between February and October 1917, grew even worse after the victory of the Bolsheviks. Transportation was in total disarray, production on the farms had dropped precipitously, people

---

[58] Quoted in Trotsky, *The Russian Revolution*, op. cit., pp. 237-238.

[59] Lenin, *Collected Works*, op. cit., Vol. XXXVI, pp. 301-302. See also the broader commentary of the editor of Lenin's *Selected Works*, Vol. VI (Moscow: Progress Publishers, 1975, revised edition), pp. 595-596; also Trotsky, *The Russian Revolution*, op. cit., pp. 285, 291.

[60] Edward H. Carr, *The Bolshevik Revolution, 1917-1923* (New York: Macmillan Company, 1953), Vol. II, pp. 2-58. See also Stefan T. Possony, *Lenin, The Compulsive Revolutionary* (Chicago: Regnery, 1964), pp. 281-293.

had fled from the cities, the black market flourished, and poverty and starvation were afflicting large areas of the country. With industry at a near standstill, money became worthless and wages were paid in kind; there was rationing even of necessities and peasants were not able to buy manufactured goods in the cities. Farmers stopped producing a surplus of grain, keeping their sowing to the minimum required to feed their families, and trying to conceal what little stock they had. The support of the peasantry for the Bolsheviks was sporadic, and it stemmed largely from the fear that the victory of the counterrevolution might result in denial of their rights to the land, which rights had been confirmed by the Soviets.

The workers also began to realize that the price paid by them for "their" revolution was exorbitant, and the results of these "expenses" very uncertain. Industrial output by 1920 was only 20 percent of what it had been before the war. The coal mines were producing one-tenth and the iron foundries only one-fourteenth of their normal output.[61] Administrative services had ground to a halt, and it was impossible to collect regular taxes. Even CHEKA (the All-Russian Extraordinary Commission), which had been brought into being six weeks after the revolution to "combat counterrevolution and sabotage," was not very successful in the economic field.[62]

In this situation, one can admit that, if his revolution was to succeed, Lenin "had to" embrace "necessary" measures of compulsion and support Trotsky's project for the conscription and militarization of factories, which was to pave the way for economic recovery. Lenin's determination allowed the revolution to develop in the form desired by the Bolsheviks. This determination, however, pushed Lenin on the road to requisitions, militarization, compulsory labor, and a struggle with workers and peasants whose interests were, at least in theory, to be represented by the Bolsheviks. All these measures, employed in the time of War Communism, had important consequences later for the organization of labor in the Soviet Union. If the revolution in the Bolshevik form was to survive, these measures were necessary. Yet, once employed, they became a precedent which, at any time, could be invoked by the party.

However, to gain substantial mass support and preserve their emotional attachment to ideological tenets, the Bolsheviks refused to proclaim this sometimes obvious dichotomy between theory and practice.[63] Their propaganda continually attempted to sustain the popular myth that the system was implementing the principles of proletarian democracy, that the working class was really in power, that its leaders were totally dedicated to the ideals

---

[61] See figures cited by Alexander A. Baykov, *The Development of the Soviet System* (Moscow: 1958), Vol. II, p. 8.

[62] Edward H. Carr, *The Russian Revolution* (New York: The Free Press, Macmillan, 1979), p. 20.

[63] See Deutscher, "Defeat in Victory," in Hendel, editor, *Soviet Crucible*, op. cit., p. 95.

of communism, and that their actions were in strict adherence to Marxism-Leninism. The alleged "flexibility" of Lenin's policy undoubtedly set the stage for the "omnipotence of the totalitarian lie" that, in the future, was to become a powerful means for regulating all realms of human activity, the means of "the total mental and moral expropriation of people."[64]

In theory, the system was based on the principle of democratic centralism; in practice, the emphasis was put on "centralism," while "democratic" elements (such as the election of delegates to congresses and the election of the party central committee) were strongly limited by the lack of adequate "democratic" control over the party authorities. Party policy, once decided, could no longer be challenged.[65]

Leninism began to live its double life. The facade of Lenin's principles of "democratic centralism," "intra-party democracy," and "dictatorship of the proletariat" was exploited by party propaganda, but it was not expected to be observed. The real totalitarian core of Leninism, purified from its pseudo-democratic rhetoric and humanitarian clichés, gave an "all conquering" power to Lenin's ideas.

At the end of his life Lenin began to realize that totalitarian excesses might result in the degeneration of the first communist state. He still did not understand where the roots of this process were, and did not believe in its irreversibility. Summing up his revolutionary experiences, he said (in his Political Report to the Eleventh Party Congress),

the machine refused to obey the hand that guided it. It was like a car that was going not in the direction the driver desired, but in the direction someone else desired; as if it were being driven by some mysterious, lawless hand, God knows whose, perhaps that of a profiteer, or of a private capitalist, or of both . . . . If we take Moscow with its 4,700 communists in responsible positions, and if we take that huge bureaucratic machine, that gigantic heap, we must ask: who is directing that heap? To tell the truth, they are not directing, they are being directed.[66]

Lenin was a pragmatist, but his pragmatism did not prevent him from believing that, in the future, facts would correspond more nearly with his theory. His biggest illusion was based on the conviction that all of the "necessary" measures which had distorted the policy of the party were temporary and could easily be renounced. The Bolshevik Party "consciously" had to sacrifice some ideals, but the retreat from the "way of deviations" was to be spontaneous. Communism itself, in a way, was to straighten out the path of the Bolsheviks, keeping individuals totally obedient and disciplined without compulsion. It was to provide new, charismatic leaders and

---

[64] See on these points, Leszek Kolakowski, *Main Currents of Marxism*, Vol. II (Oxford: Clarendon Press, 1978), p. 517; also L. Kolakowski, "Totalitarianism & Lie," *Commentary*, May 1983, p. 35.

[65] See Nettle, *The Soviet Achievement*, op. cit., p. 23.

[66] Lenin, *Collected Works*, op. cit., Vol. XXXIII, pp. 278-280.

attract the working masses of the world into adopting the Soviet philosophy. As we know, the reality diverged significantly from the theory. The revolution did not spread to the rest of the world. The collective economy proved to be inefficient. The state and the law did not wither away. And the ideal unity of individuals and society proved to be utopian. All these fallacies and failures could be traced to Lenin's political fanaticism; contrary to his expectations, they accounted for the future crisis of communism.

In sum, Lenin, a genius in the strategies of grasping power, was less successful as a politician. He particularly seemed not to realize that the revolution which Marx intended to use as a means could become an end in itself. His imagination did not appear to reach beyond the revolution nor to grasp the price which was to be paid for his single-minded devotion to one goal.

Stalin's Legacy

To accomplish revolutionary goals, the personalities of Lenin's party members had to undergo irreversible psychological transformations. Revolutionary violence and coercion in the service of overarching goals justified the lack of moral scruples. Extreme toughness and ruthlessness were considered to be consonant with "revolutionary morality," which adopted from normal human ethics nothing but the name.

The party was to give its members the illusion that they were not personally responsible for their actions. The party took responsibility for all acts committed by its members on behalf of the organization. Without the party the individual felt completely isolated and alienated from society, deprived of any sensible justification for his former activity, hated by everybody. No one depicted the psychological effects of Bolshevization on the personality of party members better than Nikolai Bukharin at the time of his trial. "And when you ask yourself," he said in his last plea, "very well, suppose you do not die; suppose by some miracle you remain alive, again what for? Isolated from everybody, an enemy of the people, in an inhuman position, completely isolated from everything that constitutes the essence of life."[67]

Georgi L. Pyatakov explained the same problem in a broader manner:

... a true Bolshevik has submerged his personality in the collectivity of "the Party" to such an extent that he can make the effort necessary to break away from his own opinions and convictions, and can honestly agree with the Party— that is the test of a true Bolshevik. There could be no life for him, outside the ranks of the Party, and he would be ready to believe that black was white, and white was black, if the Party required it. In order to become one with this great Party, he would fuse himself with it, abandon his own personality, so that there

---

[67] Quoted by Conquest in *The Great Terror*, op. cit., p. 133.

43

was no particle left inside him which was not at one with the Party, did not belong to it.[68]

Those who desired to cross the threshold of party initiation were to be prepared for all sufferings and sacrifices. They should be ready to commit any crime on behalf of the party, and finally to be disillusioned in their expectations. As Ivan Turgenev wrote in his *The Threshold*, only fools and saints had such a mentality.

Practice, unfortunately, turned out to be much more prosaic. It did not produce saints or fools exclusively but, more often, encouraged the emergence of Stalin-type personalities for whom the opportunity to indulge their ruthlessness, often little short of pure cruelty, was sufficient justification for a party career. The difficulties of war communism, the exigencies of collectivization and industrialization, and the struggles with "capitalist reaction" and internal counterrevolution, all seemed to require the presence of tough, unscrupulous individuals. In practical confrontations, this type of leader had more chance for survival than old-fashioned, Leninist intellectuals.

In this sense, Stalin, surely, was no accidental phenomenon. He represented revolutionary ideals in a less sophisticated, more vulgar form than did Trotsky, Kamenev, or even Zinoviev, but the core of his concepts was undoubtedly Leninist. Lenin taught Stalin to adopt the flexible Marxist doctrine to suit his purposes. Lenin's peculiar adherence to Marxist dogmas inevitably influenced his successors.[69] He believed that nobody but he himself properly understood Marxism. Why should Stalin be less arbitrary? Lenin practiced violence toward those who opposed the Bolsheviks, Stalin toward those who seemed to be working against his wishes. As Robert Conquest wrote, "Lenin's terror was the product of the years of war and violence, of the collapse of society and administration, the desperate acts of rulers precariously riding the flood, and fighting for control and survival. Stalin, on the contrary, attained complete control of the country at a time when general conditions were calm."[70] Yet for Stalin, terror was also "necessary," although the meaning of the word "necessary" was slightly altered. "Arbitrary behavior by one person encouraged and permitted arbitrariness in others."[71]

Just how much Stalin's most vicious acts sprang from his manner of ruling and how much they stemmed from his own psychopathic personality is nearly impossible to say. For all his ruthlessness, Lenin was motivated by

---

[68] Quoted in Leonard Schapiro, *The Communist Party of the Soviet Union* (London: Eyre & Spottiswoode, 1960), p. 381; see also Conquest, *The Great Terror, op. cit.*, p. 128.

[69] See Robert Conquest, *Where Marx Went Wrong* (London: Tom Stacey, Ltd., 1970), pp. 99-105.

[70] Conquest, *The Great Terror, op. cit.*, p. 277.

[71] This slogan, used by Khrushchev in connection with his attack on the Stalin-Beria type of politics, obviously has much broader significance. See *The Death of Stalin: An Investigation by "Monitor"* (London: 1958), p. 93.

44

ideological reasons. Stalin, on the contrary, was an unscrupulous, ambitious man. Stalin seemed to be driven predominantly by personal motives. Yet, we must also realize that in this case clear-cut distinctions between "personal" and "objective" determinants are very elusive. Both kinds of motives are usually thoroughly intertwined. It is obvious that Stalin tried to assume the appearance of the "father of the people," for more than pragmatic reasons. He seemed to believe in his historical role. Living with one's own total political cynicism is usually intolerable for anyone over a long period of time, and it is usually replaced at some point by a kind of semi-rational self-justification in an attempt to legitimize one's personal ambitions and political decisions. Stalin was no exception.

It must be admitted that, on the one hand, Stalin managed to conceal his personal motives under the cloak of Leninism with amazing success. On the other hand, the totalitarian propensities of Lenin's policy definitely opened the gate to the excesses of Stalin's epoch. Leninism paved the way for Stalinist deformations and deviations. Totalitarian methods, once adopted, could not be abandoned without jeopardizing the very existence of the entire Bolshevik regime. It is difficult to determine how great this risk was, or whether democratization of the system, if introduced in the post-revolutionary period, would really have caused the collapse of Bolshevism. The fact is that the acute awareness of such a risk, which was deeply rooted in the minds of the members of all ranks of the Bolshevik Party, made it possible for the leaders to manipulate the enormous party bureaucracy with little difficulty. Stalin especially was a master of this kind of argument. He succeeded in convincing the Bolsheviks that any change in policy would certainly lead to the fall of the party. Terror, once employed as a method of handling opposition leaders, could easily be used by the opponents against the party, should it decide upon any relaxation. In Stalin's view, only permanent terror could prevent retaliation.

Throughout the years of his rule, Stalin persuaded the members of the Central Committee to believe that there was no one who could take his place, that "any change of leadership would be extremely dangerous, and that the country must continue its present course, since to stop now or attempt a retreat would mean the loss of everything."[72] He succeeded in convincing them that, in spite of terror, only he was capable of keeping everything together.

Those who disapproved of his policy were exterminated. The others were forced to agree that collectivization had to be a rapid process rather than a gradual reform, that industrialization would achieve a miraculous transformation of the country, and that the party was surrounded by traitors and spies. Stalin, as Lenin before him, accepted only cooperation. There

---

[72] Conquest, *The Great Terror*, op. cit., p. 34.

was no room for neutrality or innocence in this system. Everybody had to share the common responsibility. Some communists still had faith in the party; some feared that the annihilation of millions of completely defenseless and innocent people would never be forgotten by society; while others, for lack of other motives, acted in accordance with an abstract loyalty to ideas to which they were simply attached and without which they could no longer exist. As Robert Conquest wrote, "their surrender was not a single and exceptional act in their career, but the calculation of a whole series of submissions to the party made in terms they knew to be 'objectively false.' "[73] And these "submissions" gradually blocked all possibility of retreat. The process of moral degradation was not immediate; it grew step by step until the moment when it became irreversible.

---

[73] Ibid., p. 124.

3.

The Phase of Denunciation

"Samizdat" and the Russian Cultural Opposition

STALIN'S DEATH resulted not only in a wave of popular unrest—revolt of East German workers in 1953, turbulence in Siberian camps soon afterward, upheavals of Hungarian and Polish workers three years later—but also in attempts to reassess the significance of communism in the Soviet bloc. Thousands of political prisoners were released from labor camps; they had had enough time to realize that some mechanisms of the system were obsolete and needed rapid modernization. "De-Stalinization," no matter how serious its concessions, undoubtedly stimulated widespread discussion over the theory and practice of communism. Stalin's death and Khrushchev's attack on the alleged "sanctities" of Stalinism deepened the process of the intellectual disintegration of Marxism-Leninism and initiated the relatively long stage of denunciation.[74]

The new opposition to Stalinist orthodoxy, predominantly intellectual, found its main expression in literature. The Soviet dissident intelligentsia sought to reveal all the crimes of the Stalinist period and expose the manipulation of public opinion and the disastrous effects of crude political interference in the spheres of science and art. Literature seemed to be a perfect method for spreading the seeds of intellectual discontent.

The Soviet regime reacted in its typical zigzag fashion. That part of the literature which corresponded with Khrushchev's criticism of Stalin's distortions was tolerated—but only up to the moment when the party realized the double-edged character of a weapon which attacked not only Stalinism but also the "heirs of Stalin." Early in 1957, Khrushchev began a cautious retreat from his de-Stalinization campaign. In a public speech he openly criticized the struggle against the principle of *partiinost* in science and literature:

. . . among the writers in our country are individuals who say: how can there be a Party guidance of literature? One writer or another may sit at his country house,

---

[74] The scope of this study does not allow for a systematic and comprehensive analysis of the history of the anti-Bolshevik opposition; we can only briefly touch upon this broad problem in an effort to emphasize a few main trends which contributed to the denunciation of the blunders and deficiencies of Soviet communism.

hatching a sniveling book, yet want it to be recognized as an expression of the sentiments of the people of our times, of all the people. Is that not a real cult of one's personality which, you see, does not want to suffer the guidance of the Party, expressing the will of millions? And such a man with his contrived book wants to rise above the Party, above the people.[75]

It was obvious that the regime by no means wanted to condemn literature which had served so far as a useful instrument for achieving state purposes, but by the middle of the 1960s, a reversal of policy, marking the end of "liberalization" in the arts, was visible. As Abraham Rothbert wrote: ". . . the publication of Yevtushenko's *The Heirs of Stalin* in October 1962 and of Nekrasov's *Both Sides of the Ocean* and Solzhenitsyn's *One Day in the Life of Ivan Denisovitch* in November was at once the high point and the turning point of de-Stalinization and liberalization in the arts."[76]

The return to restrictions on literary freedom in the Soviet Union stimulated greater activity on the part of Russian *samizdat*.[77] Banned manuscripts, retyped open letters, novels, memoirs, and leaflets began to circulate among readers who themselves distributed retyped materials among relatives and friends. As Michael Nicholson wrote, "samizdat was born out of spasmodic easing of literary controls which followed the death of Stalin and the public criticism of his dictatorship initiated by Khrushchev."[78] The spirit of Russian *samizdat* emerged from the spontaneous meetings of Russian intellectuals, mainly poets and writers, at the foot of the Maiakovskii statue on Moscow's Maiakovskii Square. Yet, this renaissance of *samizdat* was also marked by the first trials of writers. The arrest of Yuli Daniel and Andrei Siniavski in the autumn of 1965 and their trial in 1966 provoked a new wave of protests among Russian intellectuals, who demanded public access to the materials of the trial. Some of them, with Vladimir Bukovsky in the lead, were sent to psychiatric hospitals; others, like Alexander Ginzburg, Yuri Galanskov, Viacheslav Chornovil, Vera Lashkova, and Alexei Dobrovolsky were arrested.[79] "Nevertheless," wrote Andrei Amalrik, "samizdat, like the Cultural Opposition, gradually gave birth to a new, independent force which can already be regarded as a real political opposition to the regime or, at least, as a

---

[75] *Pravda*, July 2, 1959. Cited in Abraham Rothberg, *The Heirs of Stalin: Dissidence and the Soviet Regime, 1953-1970* (Ithaca, N.Y.: Cornell University Press, 1972), pp. 26-27.

[76] Ibid., p. 60.

[77] The word *"samizdat,"* which translates roughly as "Russia's underground press," is a play on words, a distortion of the name of the Soviet Publishing House *"Gosizdat."* *"Gos"* is replaced by *"sam,"* which means "self-done"—thus, published by ourselves, not by the state.

[78] Michael Nicholson, "Solzhenitsyn and Samizdat," in John B. Dunlop, Richard Haugh, and Alexis Klimoff, editors, *Alexander Solzhenitsyn: Critical Essays and Documentary Materials* (New York: Collier Books, Macmillan, 1975), p. 71.

[79] See Peter Reddaway, *Uncensored Russia: Protest and Dissent in the USSR* (New York: American Heritage Press, 1972). See also Valery Chalidze, *V. Bukovsky: Soviet Dissenter* (New York, 1976), p. 3; Vladimir Bukovsky, *To Build a Castle: My Life as a Dissenter* (New York: Viking Press, 1977), pp. 223-348; Pavel Litvinov, *The Demonstration in Pushkin Square* (Boston: Gambit, 1969).

political opposition in embryo."[80] Whatever can be said about the weakness of Russian political dissidence, it must be admitted that Russian literature in the form of a *samizdat* network and the political trials of writers and scientists revealed the mechanisms of the Soviet system, which had and have nothing in common with socialism. The Russian Cultural Opposition was an extremely important step in the process of denunciation of the real face of Bolshevism.

Revisionism and "Reform from Within"

The opposition to Stalinist orthodoxy quickly spread to other countries of the Soviet bloc. Similar patterns of dissidence developed within other communist parties. Intellectual discussions over basic Marxist tenets united dissidents of all sorts who shared the universal mood of frustration and discontent and were ready to examine the possibility of "revision" of Marxism-Leninism and adaptation of its healthy core to recent social trends. They opposed the petrification and fossilization of Marxism but could scarcely agree as to which ideas really belonged to the "healthy core" of scientific communism. Revisionism did not intend to depart from Marxism; its proponents wanted to "purge communism of abuses," "reform Marxism," and "go back to sources."[81] Revisionism did not attack basic socialist dogmas. It criticized the role of party ideology, contributing to its disintegration, but still defended the possibility of "reform from within." Revisionists believed in the socialist future of Soviet bloc countries, in the possibility of "socialism with a human face"; almost all were determined to retain the communist party domination of their countries. Even the most militant revisionists, highly critical of their communist party's policies, manifested their attachment to socialism and believed that they would be able to offer an alternative and viable socialist political program.

The term "revisionism" did not have a very clear meaning. As Leszek Kolakowski wrote:

From the second half of the 1950s the term "revisionism" was used by the party authorities and official ideologists in Communist countries to stigmatize those who, while remaining party members or Marxists, attacked various Communist dogmas. No precise meaning was attached to it, or indeed to the label of "dogmatism" affixed to party "conservatives" who opposed the post-Stalin reforms, but as a rule the term "revisionism" connoted democratic and rational tendencies.[82]

---

[80] Andrei Amalrik, *Will the Soviet Union Survive Until 1984?* (New York: Harper & Row, 1970), pp. 9-10.

[81] Kolakowski, *Main Currents in Marxism*, Vol. III, op. cit., p. 487.

[82] Ibid., pp. 456-457.

The division among the dogmatic and revisionist wings of the party was sometimes purposefully obliterated. Paradoxically, both groups wanted to be concurrently orthodox and reformist, both stressed their Marxist-Leninist background and the desire to introduce some "adjustments." They varied in their opinions as to the scope of reform, but the term "reform" was heard everywhere. Dogmatic hardliners tried to conceal their "reactionism" behind reformist clichés, while revisionists manifested their attachment to the "healthy" roots of Marxism-Leninism. In fact, dogmatists were interested mainly in replacing one hardliner with another—not with introducing reformers into positions of power. Their "reformist" approach was occasioned mostly by fear for their own fate. Revisionists questioned the thesis that errors made in the period of "deviations" were exclusively tactical, and they opted for a deep reform of party policy.[83] They wanted to reveal ideological manipulation by the Soviet regime, to point out that Marxist theory was replaced by propaganda which selectively exposed, when it was convenient, only certain aspects of Marxism-Leninism.

Revisionists, divided by internal debates and animosities, did not produce a coherent doctrine. As Jakub Karpinski correctly remarked, "It is perhaps easier to assemble a list of persons who have been described as revisionists than to compile a list of revisionist views."[84] Dissident groups did not adopt definite organizational forms, but regarded themselves as a movement mostly because of common opposition to the conservative ruling elite. Yet, despite this disunity of the dissident movement, it was possible to distinguish in it a few distinct factions which concentrated their attention either on political or economic reforms or on a struggle for basic human rights.

Political reformers wanted to bring about a general democratization of public life, to change relations between the communist party and the public, and to increase popular participation in policymaking processes. Political revisionists called for intra-party democracy and pluralization of political life. They criticized the dictatorship of the party which, in Lenin's concept, was to be only a temporary measure—whereas, in fact, the rule of the party vanguard has never been relaxed.

Economic revisionists concentrated on criticism of the inefficiency of socialist economic management. They did not attack the basic dogma of public property, but rather advocated increasing the role of market factors, improving the planning system, introducing new production incentives, and stimulating the interest of workers and managers in qualitative (not only quantitative) production efforts. Some revisionists supported a spontaneous

---

[83] See Michael Gamarnikov, "Poland: Political Pluralism in a One-Party State," *Problems of Communism*, July-August, 1967, pp. 3-4.

[84] Jakub Karpinski, *Count-down: The Polish Upheavals of 1956, 1958, 1970, 1976, 1980. . . .* (New York: Kartz-Cohl Publishers, 1982), p. 108.

movement toward the dissolution of collective farms, and predicted the end of collectivization.

Other revisionists concentrated their activity on the struggle for human rights and intellectual freedom, particularly demanding an increase in freedom of expression, the removal of political restrictions on independent thinking, and a greater emphasis on the rule of law.[85]

Gradually the optimistic vision of an introduction of widespread reforms turned out to be nothing but a series of disappointments. When the Soviets invaded Hungary in 1956, the optimism of believers in the "new deal" was dealt a shattering blow. After popular unrest in Budapest and in Poland was suppressed, the Soviet regime and authorities of the satellite countries turned their attention to strengthening party discipline and purging dissenters. The Kremlin supported a massive campaign which was launched in all countries of the bloc and resulted in further disarray of the revisionist movement, which had never been very well integrated. The regime quickly succeeded in its strategy of silencing the most militant intellectuals. The majority of well-known dissenters were arrested, sent abroad, assigned to Soviet labor camps or psychiatric hospitals, or simply assimilated by the system. The handful of remaining active dissidents concentrated their attention on the defense of human rights and a struggle for justice and enforcement of the law. Intellectual freedom was a central demand of dissident intellectuals of the late 1950s and early 1960s.

In Poland, which avoided a Soviet invasion, an optimistic faith in the liberal policy of Gomulka's new government lasted a little longer. Yet, in 1957, Gomulka proclaimed that revisionism was worse than the distortions of Stalinism. In the summer of that year, *Po prostu (To Put It Plainly)*, a weekly magazine published by students and young intelligentsia and generally regarded as a center of Polish revisionism, was shut down. The series of student demonstrations which followed this decision was quickly suppressed. The concept of a gradual transformation of the corroded system was obviously a failure. Revisionists soon discovered that, despite de-Stalinization, the main institutions of the Soviet system remained essentially Stalinist. Disappointed and demoralized, some young rebels joined the group of party cynics. Others needed more time to develop new projects and plans.

"Reform from Without"

The atmosphere of disappointment in the late 1950s furthered the erosion of intellectual belief in the value of the communist "historic mission." The Soviet invasion of Hungary and the subsequent brutal repression seemed

---

[85] See Kolakowski, *Main Currents of Marxism*, Vol. III, op. cit., p. 457.

to confirm the thesis that Bolshevism and socialism have few attributes in common. The debate over this view opened a new phase in the "process of denunciation."

Advocates of this thesis still differed in their opinions as to whether Bolshevism could be transformed into "genuine socialism" without a new revolution. The most moderate admitted that the gulf between "genuine" Marxism and Bolshevism in its recent shape had increased, but they (former followers of George Lukacs from the "Petofi Circle") still emphasized their fidelity to socialism, opposition to pluralism, and readiness to keep reforms within the framework of Marxism.[86] Rudolf Bahro wrote: "Today the peoples of the Soviet Union and the East European countries are recognizing more and more that the new system only corresponds in a small way to the principles it proclaims, betraying its own goals and no longer achieving anything new."[87]

Despite this criticism, the quest for "the third (but still socialist) way" found especially strong support from an East German anti-Stalinist opposition, from W. Harich to Robert Havemann and Rudolf Bahro.[88] German revisionists remained active as an intracommunist opposition longer than the Poles or Czechs. Even after 1968, when the great majority of Polish and Czech dissidents shared the opinion of Kolakowski that the defeat of "the Prague Spring" marked the end of revisionism for all of Europe, German intellectuals professing revisionist ideas still considered the possibility of "reform from within." They still agreed with Bahro's view that the idea of intracommunist criticism of the party apparatus might be successful, and the future of Eastern Europe rested in a gradual but basic reform of the present political system.[89] Bahro criticized the conception of party pluralism, which seemed to him "to be an anarchistic piece of thoughtlessness, which completely misconstrues the concrete historical materials in our countries."[90] He himself stressed the necessity of a "democratic revolution against politbureaucracy" but by "revolution" he meant attempts at creation of a new communist league, internationalization of the struggle of the antibureau-

---

[86] Kolakowski suggests that "the much more orthodox character of Hungarian revisionism was the reason why it became so detached from the movement of popular discontent [and] the revisionists were unable to keep the attack on the party within bounds; the result was a mass protest, expressly anti-Communist in character, leading to the collapse of the party and to Soviet invasion." Ibid., p. 464.

[87] Rudolf Bahro, Introduction to "The Alternative in Eastern Europe," published in *The Case of Rudolf Bahro: A Socialist in an East German Prison* (Nottingham, England: Russell Press, Ltd., 1979), p. 9.

[88] See H. Weber, "The Third Way: Bahro's Place in the Tradition of Anti-Stalinist Opposition," in Ulf Wolter, editor, *Rudolf Bahro: Critical Responses* (Armonk, N.Y.: M.E. Sharpe, 1980), pp. 3-21.

[89] See *The Case of Rudolf Bahro*, op. cit., p. 5; see also Jiri Pelikan, "Bahro's Ideas on Change in Eastern Europe," in Wolter, editor, *Rudolf Bahro: Critical Responses*, op. cit., p. 171.

[90] Rudolf Bahro, *The Alternative in Eastern Europe* (London: NLB, 1978), p. 350.

cratic opposition, and formation of parallel structures alongside the official institutions which would concentrate their activity especially on the struggle for civil rights. His conclusion was that "the politbureaucracy must be disarmed, the domination of the apparatus over society removed, the relationship between society and state newly arranged, and the communist movement newly constituted. . . ."[91] Yet he left no doubts as to his belief that the "new alternative" was "maturing in the womb of actually existing socialism."[92]

In the early 1960s, Czech and Polish revisionists took a step forward. Gradually they began to realize that the deficiencies, discussed so broadly, had become permanent components of communist regimes. The awareness that a process of further deterioration of the system was inevitable gradually spread over intellectual circles in Eastern Europe. Alexander Solzhenitsyn's skepticism regarding the reformative capability of the communist system was widely shared.[93] It was pointed out that deviations from the principles of democratic socialism and suppression of basic civil liberties helped communist elites survive and enabled them to maintain power, but also resulted in the irreversible degeneration of the whole system. It is this burden that the communists must bear and will bear until the end of their rule. The concept of communist democracy seemed more and more to be (using Kolakowski's expression) a kind of "boiling ice." The process of "education" was long, and a watchful observer could note successive waves of optimism and pessimism, periods of an explicit anticommunist reaction followed by a retreat from the theory of the "irreversible fallacies" of communism. Let us follow the main stages of this process.

During 1963 and 1964, the Gomulka regime resumed in Poland a temporarily suspended (after the "Polish October" of 1956) policy of restricting democratic rights. It shut down the leading liberal weeklies, *Nowa Kultura* and *Przeglad Kulturalny*. In March 1964, a group of Polish intellectuals sent a *Letter of 34* to the then Premier, Jozef Cyrankiewicz, protesting political restrictions on independent thinking, requesting more freedom of expression, and criticizing the party's control over academic works. At the same time a party-sponsored club, which served as a forum for discussions of the basic tenets of Marxism, was dissolved.

These events led two young intellectuals from Warsaw University, Jacek Kuron and Karol Modzelewski, to submit *An Open Letter to Communist Party Members* to the Warsaw University branch of the Polish United Workers

---

[91] Ibid., pp. 311-312.

[92] Ibid., p. 14.

[93] As Daniel Singer wrote: " . . . in fairness, it must be added that Solzhenitsyn was among the first—long before the Soviet intervention in Czechoslovakia—to perceive the intrinsic inability of the regime to move beyond certain boundaries." Daniel Singer, *The Road to Gdansk: Poland and the USSR* (New York: Monthly Review Press, 1982), p. 48.

Party,[94] in which they openly condemned the ruling elite for exploitation of the workers. In their pessimistic assessment of events since October 1956, they stressed that the apparent transformation did not affect the basic and most corroded structures of the system. Kuron and Modzelewski argued that Poland was ruled in a despotic way by a new party bureaucracy which was responsible for the deep economic and social crisis. "This Party-state power elite, free of any social control and able independently to make all key economic decisions of nationwide importance (as well as all political decisions), we shall call the central political bureaucracy."[95]

Kuron and Modzelewski still attempted to analyze the problem in terms of the Marxist "class conflict" and the dependence of the superstructure on the relations of production. Communist society, they argued, is divided into two fundamentally opposed classes: the exploited working class and the exploiting class of the political bureaucracy. A dictatorship of the party elite, which was necessary in the phase of rapid industrialization, became superfluous in more developed socialist countries. Modern societies need pluralization of political life; "the working class must organize itself along multiparty lines."[96] Kuron and Modzelewski predicted that the contradictions between modern productive forces and obsolete political organization would result in an antibureaucratic revolution: "In view of the impossibility of overcoming the crisis within the framework of the bureaucratic system, revolution is inevitable."[97]

Kuron and Modzelewski attempted to analyze socialism in the same way that Marx analyzed capitalism, as a social formation in which a superstructure is dependent on the relations of production. They still used Marxist language and appealed to socialist theory, but their conclusions were different from those of the revisionists of the middle 1950s. A change still seemed to be possible, but it was not to come from within the communist party. Bolshevism had to be destroyed by revolution and then replaced by a totally new kind of "real socialism" to be introduced through the pressure of revolting masses.

The issue of political pluralism, which was to be a main characteristic of "genuine socialism," was raised also by other Polish intellectuals, with Kolakowski at the head. In his October 1966 address to mark the tenth anniversary of Gomulka's post-Stalinist regime, Kolakowski, a professor of Marx-

---

[94] On November 14, 1964, police searched the home of Karol Modzelewski (whose father was, *note bene*, a top-ranking party official) and uncovered an unfinished manuscript of the letter. At the end of November, Modzelewski and Kuron released the text of their letter, and in 1965 they were tried and sentenced to prison for three and three-and-a-half years, respectively.

[95] Jacek Kuron and Karol Modzelewski, *Solidarnosc: The Missing Link? The Classic Open Letter to the Party by Jacek Kuron and Karol Modzelewski*, with a new introduction by Colin Barker (London: Bookmarks, 1982), p. 15.

[96] Ibid., p. 74.

[97] Ibid., p. 66.

54

ist philosophy, former editor of the journal *Po Prostu,* and Poland's most famous dissident intellectual, offered a full reassessment of the intellectual hopes and disappointments of the Polish intelligentsia. He challenged the openly authoritarian behavior of the party elite, the inept economic decisions, the abuses of the police system, and all permanent limitations on intellectual freedom. "Socialism," concluded Kolakowski, "can and must assimilate democratic pluralism."[98]

The events of the late 1960s had a fundamental significance for the education of a whole generation of Polish intellectuals. Until 1968 most of them believed that with time even the most orthodox communist leaders would be able to see the crisis of their model and would try, pressed by social forces from outside the party, to modify it. The experience of the late 1960s strongly undermined this belief.

The thesis that Bolshevism should not be identified with socialism and that, this being so, a reform "from within" the existing communist party would have to be replaced by a reform "from without," also found its expression in the Czech dissident movement. Czech intellectuals stressed, perhaps more strongly than Polish writers and scholars, their attachment to socialism, but they also admitted that the existence of an opposition faction within the party did not guarantee democratic transformations.

On June 27, 1968, four Czechoslovak periodicals published an article entitled, "2000 Words to Workers, Farmers, Officials, Scientists, Artists, and Everyone." Written by Ludvik Vaculik but endorsed by other prominent Czech intellectuals, the article was soon recognized as a manifesto which pointed to the direction for political change. The tone of "2000 Words" was less militant than that of the *Open Letter* of Kuron and Modzelewski. Vaculik criticized the policies of the Czechoslovak Communist Party, but also emphasized the significance of socialism which was "hopefully accepted by the majority of the nation."[99] He also proclaimed a "trust of signatories" in the forthcoming process of democratization to be steered by the Communist Party. Vaculik wrote: "From the beginning of the current year, we have been taking part in a revival process of democratization. That it began in the Communist party must be acknowledged."[100]

The other Czech intellectuals went further in their criticism of communist rule. In a lecture at the Philosophical Faculty of Charles University in Prague, Professor I. Svitak asserted that "achieving democratic socialism is contingent upon the liquidation of the mechanisms of totalitarian dictatorship and the totalitarian way of thinking. Totalitarian dictatorship," he concluded,

---

[98] See Gamarnikov, "Poland . . . ," *Problems of Communism,* op. cit., pp. 7-8.

[99] *Literarni Listy,* June 27, 1968; for the complete text, see Robin A. Remington, editor, *Winter in Prague: Documents on Czechoslovak Communism in Crisis,* with an introduction by William E. Griffith (Cambridge, Mass.: The MIT Press, 1969), p. 196.

[100] Ibid., p. 198.

"is our enemy Number One."[101] Svitak explicitly emphasized that Czechs must realize the difference between a revolution and a revolt:

A revolution means structural social changes in class relations, in the relations between economy and policy, and in the structure of the mechanisms of power. A revolt is an exchange of teams and does not affect structural relations and questions. . . . We are profoundly indifferent to the latter possibility. We have no reason to be enthusiastic about an exchange of persons.[102]

The criticism of the young Czech playwright, Vaclav Havel, was even more blatant. In his article, "On the Subject of Opposition," published in *Literarni Listy*, he dismissed "as illusory the assumption that internal democratization of the leading party (willingness to tolerate something like internal party opposition) offers a sufficient guarantee of democracy."[103] Democracy, in Havel's view, is a matter not of faith but of guarantees, and the present political system not only is unable to provide any guarantee but is totally compromised by decades of slavish docility to a small Bolshevik elite.[104]

Toward a Political Opposition

The failure of the "Prague Spring" and student unrest in Poland in 1968 hastened the erosion of intellectual belief in communism but also resulted in further political fragmentation of the dissident movement. Many purged academics left both countries, and remaining dissidents acted in small, often isolated groups. The revisionist movement in Czechoslovakia was virtually destroyed by the Soviet invasion. In Poland, the lack of direct Soviet intervention, combined with the particularly strong traditions of national resistance to Russian expansionism, led to major changes in the dissidents' approach to communism and the dictatorship of the Communist Party. Dissidence was transformed into political opposition, and in this respect Poland moved in a direction distinctly different from the other socialist countries.

The failure of student unrest in Poland activated more militant and clearly anticommunist groups, which did not confine their agenda to the defense of human rights, but openly demanded the independence of Poland and other satellite countries and stressed the necessity of a "national road to democracy." Their members planned demonstrations of "active protest"

---

[101] Ibid., p. 80.
[102] Ibid., pp. 78-79.
[103] Ibid., p. 65.
[104] Ibid., p. 63.

which were to consist mostly in the total destruction of symbols of cooperation and friendship with the Soviet Union.[105]

The events of 1968, followed by the new wave of popular unrest in 1970, resulted in the intra-party shifts and purges which elevated the pragmatically oriented clique of Edward Gierek. These changes revealed the political, as opposed to the ideological, nature of all party factional maneuvers, and as such were also very instructive for Polish dissenters. And, accompanying the fascinating moves of Gierek's team, his economic reforms seemed to be, at least, promising. After the failure of the Czechoslovak experiment in socialist democratization, Gierek's project for "economic recovery" again aroused a wave of public optimism.

Gierek's government, having at its disposal considerable amounts of foreign currency obtained through unrestricted Western loans, decided on rapid industrialization of the country. The regime assumed that the rate of Western inflation and the rapid development of Polish industry would make possible the swift amortization of investments and repayment of loans.

This is not the place to produce a detailed examination of Poland's vast economic problems. What we can safely assert is that the regime erred. The Polish economy, based mainly on agriculture, was unable to change its character quickly. Industry was incapable of any swift expansion. Gierek's government could not provide experts capable of coordinating the different branches of the economy, much less such a drastic transition. The party leaders' arbitrary decisions, frequently altered, became ridiculous. The regime's expectations about Western inflation rates were unfulfilled. In the end, Gierek's policies resulted in the widespread collapse of Polish agriculture, the disorganization of industry, rampant inflation, and shortages of basic commodities.

By the mid-1970s, the failure of the program of "economic recovery" was broadly heralded by Polish economists, but their warnings were totally disregarded by the authorities. The announcement of a major increase in food prices on June 24, 1976, produced an increase in social tension and a new wave of unrest. In Radom, fire was set to the party committee building. In the Ursus truck plant near Warsaw, workers ripped apart an important train line; as a result, hundreds of workers were arrested and lost their jobs. The events of 1976 forced the Polish intellectual opposition to reassess its program.

It has been remarked that much of the success of Polish governmental policy has stemmed from a skillful manipulation of the attitudes of workers and intelligentsia whose interests were proclaimed by party propaganda to

---

[105] The *Ruch* (Movement) group planned to set fire to the Lenin Museum in Poronin. The Kowalczyk brothers destroyed the auditorium of the Opole Higher School of Education. For more details of these actions, see Jakub Karpinski, *Count-down* . . . , op. cit., pp. 153-155.

be basically antagonistic. Both social groups have been purposefully set against each other. This political strategy was especially visible in 1968 when, thanks to party maneuvers, support of the non-intellectual population for protesting students remained insignificant and often the attitudes of workers were even openly hostile. The party mobilized worker-activists to help put down student demonstrations. Party propagandists tried to convince workers that the country faced nothing but a wave of "hooliganism." Party activists promptly "revealed" the alleged "conspiracy" which existed behind the student protests: "healthy" communist youths were corrupted by a "Jewish plot" and by "reactionaries." In 1970, students in turn did not support the workers' struggles with Gomulka's regime, and generally remained passive observers of events.

In the middle 1970s, the approach of Polish intellectuals to the problem of cooperation with workers underwent a significant change. The term "genuine socialism" was still one of the objectives mentioned in the programs of the Polish opposition. Yet a watchful observer could easily come to the conclusion that the leaders of the opposition were referring to the "socialist perspective" of the country merely for tactical and purely pragmatic reasons. They realized that, once a social system based on the collective ownership of the means of production has been introduced, a return to private control of production is hardly feasible. Their attention shifted to the issue of parliamentary democracy, pluralization of society, sovereignty of the state, and coordination of the common, nationwide struggle against totalitarianism. The term "dissidence" was more and more frequently replaced by "political opposition." This designation was still vague, but it more accurately expressed the endeavor to free the anti-Bolshevik movement from the old Marxist sectarianism and to go beyond the traditional policies of the intra-communist opposition. In his *Thoughts on a Program of Action*, in November 1976, Jacek Kuron wrote: " . . . for a political opposition I regard all these people who consciously and actively oppose totalitarianism and stand up for the sovereignty of the Polish nation and the Polish state."[106]

Former Marxists, if they wanted to be realists, had to follow public opinion, which more and more became indifferent to ideological clichés. An ordinary citizen, when asked what he meant by socialism, used to answer that he knew nothing about socialism, but that he could describe precisely what a decent standard of living in a normal, civilized European country means.

On September 23, 1976, fourteen persons signed a declaration which announced the creation of a quasi-official organization—the Workers' Defense Committee (KOR). A year later KOR changed its name to the Committee for Social Self-Defense KOR (KSS KOR). KOR attacked the state monopoly of information and censorship, criticized the dictatorship of the party elite,

---

[106] Jacek Kuron, *Mysli o Programie Dzialanie* (Niezalezna Oficyna Wydawnicza, 1976), p. 5.

proclaimed a struggle against all forms of state repression and illegality, and called for full protection of human and civil rights in Poland. The founding group of intellectuals, including Kuron, Adam Michnik, and Edward Lipinski, proclaimed:

We were ashamed that the intelligentsia had been silent in 1970 and 1971, and we wanted to restore its good name. After the brutal suppression of workers' strikes and demonstrations, thousands of workers all over Poland found themselves without jobs. Police stations were full. Trials began at Ursus and Radom. KOR set itself the aim of organizing financial help for those dismissed from work and the families of the imprisoned; of offering legal and—when necessary—medical help; of fighting for freedom for the imprisoned and jobs for the unemployed.[107]

New organizations (Young Poland Movement, Committee of an Agreement for the Self-Determination of the Nation, and Confederation of Independent Poland), all of which put emphasis on the issue of Poland's independence, appeared in the late 1970s. The leaders of those organizations tried to initiate an agreement with the Czech Chartists and, in this way, to begin the internationalization of the movement.

Through the battle for democratic freedoms, the Polish intellectual opposition began gradually to form a timid political program.[108] The ideological, economic, and moral collapse of the system was broadly publicized, and a major effort was made to make the general public—beyond the ranks of the intelligentsia—aware of the permanency of this crisis. Political awakening especially of the workers seemed to be more and more important. The new opposition demanded the right to strike for workers, the right to debate and to organize independent trade unions. The first illegal unions were formed in Radom in 1977, and then in the mining districts of Silesia and along the Baltic Coast in 1978. Clandestine journals, like *The Worker*, *The Outpost*, *Progress*, and *The Voice* gained greater influence.[109] In the summer of 1979, *The Worker* printed a *Charter of Workers Rights*, which was to offer a rough platform for further discussion of workers' grievances. The leaders of the movement introduced a series of lectures throughout the country commonly called the "Flying University." Seminars, organized mostly in private apartments, were designed to have a galvanizing impact on the young generation. Meetings and lectures were often broken up by police, and their participants were kept imprisoned for a few days or even weeks, but the social ferment which grew from these activities soon produced results. The weak links between Polish workers and intellectuals were

---

[107] Cited in Lawrence Weschler, *Solidarity: Poland in the Season of its Passion* (New York: Simon & Schuster, 1982), pp. 163-164.

[108] See Jacek Kuron, *Zasady Ideowe, Mysli o Programie Dzialania, Uwagi o Strukturze Ruchu Demokratycznego* (Paryz: 1978).

[109] See Karpinski, *Count-down . . .* , op. cit., pp. 199-201.

strengthened, the need for cooperation was better understood, and common values were manifested. This embryonic movement turned out to be extremely important in the events of the Polish summer of 1980.

Poland was entering a new stage of crisis—the stage of public awareness—which remained until recently an exclusively Polish stage. For the Communist Party, which was accustomed to manipulating the mood of the people and putting its own leaders on the crest of a popular wave, this new opposition coalition became a serious challenge.

4.
The Phase of Awareness

Cultural and Religious Roots of the Polish Crisis of the 1980s

THE HISTORY of Solidarity is well known in the West. In the last two or three years, accounts of the Polish strikes and of the confrontations of various sectors of Polish society with the communist regime have been presented in at least twenty serious monographic works published in English, French, German, Russian, and Polish.[110] I have participated in recent years in dozens of international conferences dealing with the consecutive Polish upheavals of 1956, 1968, 1970, 1976 and 1980, and had frequently heard the comment that Western journalists, scholars, and political commentators know a great deal about the Polish unrest in the last 25 years, but still lack an answer to the basic questions: Why has the turbulence occurred mostly in Poland? Why does Poland always seem to be the powder keg of the Soviet bloc?

These questions have not only puzzled Western political observers, but they have also been widely discussed in Polish communist circles. In the late 1970s, the Polish government promoted extensive research on Poland's

---

[110] N. Neal Ascherson, *The Polish August* (London: Allen Lane, 1981); *August 1980: The Strikes in Poland* (Munich: Radio Free Europe Research, 1980); *The Book of Lech Walesa* (New York: Simon & Schuster, 1982); Jean Offredo, *Lech Walesa ou l'été polonais* (Paris: Cana-Le Corre, 1981); Karpinski, *Count-down. . . .* , op. cit.; Jean-Marie Charpentier, *Solidarnosc; un an de luttes sociales en Pologne* (Paris: Montholon Services, 1981); Michael Dobs, *Poland, Solidarity, Walesa* (New York: McGraw-Hill, 1981); Robert Eringer, *Strike for Freedom* (New York: Dodd, Mead, 1982); Jule Gatter-Klenk, *Vielleicht auf Knien, aber vorwarts* (Konigstein/Ts.: Atheneum, 1981); Jean-Louis Gazignaire, *Lech Walesa-l'espoir* (Paris: Edition du Guepard, 1981); *Gdansk, La Memoire Ouvrière 1970-1980* (Paris: François Maspero, 1982); *Kak Nachinalas 'Solidarnost'* (English title: How Solidarity Was Born) (London: Overseas Publications Interchange, 1981); Denis Macshane, *Solidarity* (Nottingham, England: Spokesman, 1981); Leszek Moczulski, *Revolution With Revolution* (Menlo Park, Calif.: California Center for the Study of Opposition in Poland, 1982); Oliver McDonald, editor, *The Polish August: Documents from the Beginnings of the Polish Workers Rebellion* (San Francisco, Calif.: Ztangi Press, 1981); Robert Polet, *The Polish Summer* (London: War Resisters International, 1981); Jean-Ives Potel, *The Promise of Solidarity* (New York: Praeger, 1982); Peter Raina, *Independent Social Movements in Poland* (London: London School of Economics and Political Science, 1981); Anna Sabbat, *Poland, A Chronology of Events, July-November 1980* (Munich: Radio Free Europe Research, 1981); Stan Persky and Henry Flam, editors, *The Solidarity Sourcebook* (Vancouver, B.C.: New Books, 1982); Stanislaw Starski, *Class Struggle in Classless Poland* (Boston: South End Press, 1982); Leszek Szymanski, *Candle for Poland* (San Bernardino, Calif.: Borgo Press, 1982).

current political culture. The official report, completed in 1979,[111] dealt, among other things, with the historical background of Poland's political culture and attempted to reveal and explain the attitudes that led to fundamental opposition to the communist state. Although Polish culture is very fluid, the study showed, there are some relatively stable components and attributes that constitute the "national character." The research indicated that there are four distinct characteristics that, in the view of the Poles themselves, typify and describe the Polish people as a whole. First, the Poles are romantics. Second, they are always ready to express their opinions—an individualism that has often led them to oppose governments, especially alien authorities whose policies and practices justified a lack of confidence in their good faith and concern for the public weal. Third, Poles admire democracy. Fourth, they are a religious people, strongly attached to Catholicism.

This study of Polish political culture demonstrated conclusively that these attributes of the national character are antithetical to the existing political system and incompatible with communism.

Obedience has always been the preeminent attitude required by any communist party. The communist police state and its system of permanent terror are dependent upon a "system of prophylaxis"—incited, artificial tensions and preventive punishment. Yet, to implement it, the government must be able to count on predictable, stable social attitudes—a condition that by and large does not exist in Poland.

Polish romanticism (to simplify the highly controversial concept somewhat) can be understood as the permanent readiness of a people to sacrifice personal safety and pleasures in defense of religion, national identity, culture, tradition, and liberty. Poles are prepared to make these sacrifices even in situations in which an ultimate struggle seems to offer no rational chance for success. It is not necessary here to probe deeply the question of what are the historical benefits and disadvantages of Polish romanticism. This balance, frequently examined in the past, has always been highly debatable. It is enough to say that recent studies confirm that many Poles still believe that romanticism is an attribute of their national mentality. Being guided by a set of "romantic" attitudes does not mean that Poles are habituated to risking their lives lightly or disregarding the values of a peaceable lifestyle which are commonly respected by citizens of other nations. It means, rather, that a difference between "existence" and "life" is deeply rooted in the consciousness of Poles. Many of them still, as in the nineteenth century, believe that life is priceless, but existence has a measured value. Survival

---

[111] Only fragments of the materials on which the report was based were published. See Rett Ludwikowski, *Polska Kultura Polityczna Tradycje, Mity i Wspolczesnosc* (Wroclaw: Zaklad Narodowy in. Ossolinskich, 1980).

makes sense only in certain circumstances. It is very typical—as foreign visitors in Poland stress frequently—that the slogan *"vivre pour le vivre"* (life just for living), promoted by West European existentialism, has never been popular in Poland. It does not mean, of course, that all Poles are romantics or that citizens of other nations never view life in this way. It means that in Poland these attitudes are more perceptible, more pervasive than in other countries. If the term "national character" is to have any meaning, it can be understood only as a set of attitudes, characteristics, and mental predispositions, determined by the unique historical experience of a nation and its people and present in great intensity in the consciousness of the current generation of its citizens. So, to conclude, if we juxtapose the romantic mentality model (with all its unpredictable, unstable, atypical attitudes) with the expectations of a totalitarian state, we can easily appreciate how incompatible the attributes of the Polish national character are with the communist system.

The report showed that Poles are individualists, intractable, naturally opposed to the typical methods of communist regimes, which strive to transform their societies into collections of isolated, dull, and opinionless individuals. Communism has always been represented as a complex of dogmas interpretable only by a specially qualified party elite. Individuals seeking truth, freedom of speech, and open presentation of views have always been suppressed. Many sociological studies emphasize the fact that compliance and conformity cannot be included among the main characteristics of the typical Pole. Poles are inclined to exaggerate rather than obscure the differences in their opinions and outlooks. As Winston Churchill often remarked, "Where there are two Poles, there are three opinions." Whatever the historical consequences of Polish individualism have been, it is a fact that in a country where communism was presented as a sacred and ultimate dogma, Poles were born revisionists and their creed of individualism inevitably had to threaten the Polish Communist Party.

The individualism of Poles found its strongest expression perhaps in Polish aspirations for an independent state, and in the strongly manifested conviction that each Pole has a right to participate in the governance of his own country. Traditions of the sovereign Polish state are deeply rooted in Polish political culture. Poles are not believers in the infallibility of democracy; the traditions of their own "nobleman's democracy," established in the sixteenth century, proved that the democratic system has both advantages and disadvantages. Yet, they are ready to acknowledge that democracy, as Winston Churchill used to say, is "the worst form of government, except for all the other forms." The younger generation of Poles is especially inclined to assert that the term "democracy" as used in the communist system is only a slogan, nothing but a cliché. Individualism strengthened their resistance to all forms of "collective mentality" and contributed to the more open (than in other countries of the Soviet bloc) manifestation of admiration for so-called formal democracy, i.e., Western democracy.

The strong attachment of Poles to Catholicism is the fourth of the major characteristics shaping recent Polish political culture, and by far the most important of them. Polish Catholicism obviously does not accord with the atheism sponsored by Marxism-Leninism. A strong Catholic Church has always been an obstacle for communists striving to liquidate all unsanctioned structures that could strengthen individuals in their struggle against the party and communist government. Yet, despite that, Catholic Poland, with the most fervently religious society in Europe—far more so than those of Spain and Italy—exists in the middle of the communist bloc. The contribution of the Church to the process of creating a common awareness of the degeneration of communist regimes demands special emphasis. Because of the Church's authority and Poland's special attachment to religion, the Poles may be the victims of communism, but they will never be its obedient children.

The Phase of Awareness

The appearance of Polish Solidarity in 1980 startled even the most careful observers of Polish politics. Periods of popular unrest were nothing new in countries of the Soviet bloc, but an independent trade union certainly did not accord with socialist realism. Hardly anyone anticipated such a turn of events. Western commentators predicted a reshuffling of the ruling clique in the Polish Political Bureau rather than profound social and political changes. Previous political shifts had usually been accomplished with the "assistance" of workers who themselves helped to elevate a new elite to power. Gierek's opponents in the Politburo could reasonably expect in 1980 that such techniques might succeed again.

But history did not repeat itself in Poland. Every successive purge of party ranks increased the circle of dissidents who could not be assimilated into the system and were aware of the irreversible degeneration of communism. With the assistance of intellectuals outside the party and of traditionally anticommunist clerics, the next stage of the crisis of communism was prepared—the stage in which the permanent weaknesses of the system became common knowledge. It was a real shock for the Polish communist bureaucrats to face a well-organized and determined movement which was ready to fight for real participation in public decisions.

Without "Polish romanticism," something like Solidarity probably could not have appeared under the communist regime. Yet it must also be admitted that this romantic optimism helped to strengthen the public conviction that the most important battle was won when the independent trade union movement was created. That optimism led the general public to overestimate the spontaneity of the movement in August 1980, and to attach insufficient importance to the objective causes of the workers' restlessness: the troubles of the Polish economy, the temporary weakness of an internally quarreling party, and the government's strategy of inciting artificial tensions in society (which failed in 1980, but in the past had usually set off social upheavals before the people were adequately organized). The leaders of Solidarity and Polish society had finished only the first lessons in their course on the "nature of totalitarianism."

The atmosphere of 1980 was generally optimistic and reformist. The public had reached the stage of awareness of the crisis of communism; yet it still did not accept the thesis that the crisis was irreversible. The people realized that the corrupt communist elite would not introduce any real changes, but they still believed that reforms could be forced on the ruling clique by rebellious masses who might later somehow assume the reins of government.

The general populace, represented by the independent trade union, did not manifest anticommunist attitudes in 1980. Public criticism was leveled at the undemocratic methods of party politics, the abuses of the ruling elite, and the inefficient economic system. The union's bulletins and pamphlets questioned the basic principles of communism, but Solidarity did not advance an openly anticommunist position.

The union strove for democratic changes in the country and demanded formal registration of Solidarity and permission to organize a Rural Solidarity among the peasants. Union leaders tried to gain control of industry, so that they might reveal the enormous corruption of high-ranking party members, and sought access to the mass media.

The public quickly learned of the restrictive mechanisms of the communist system. Solidarity activists soon began to understand that in a totalitarian state, which has monopoly control not only over political, social, and economic spheres, but also over private and personal life, it is not possible to address social problems without first gaining influence over political and economic issues. They realized that they would gain nothing in the social sphere, with which the trade unions are primarily concerned, without the actual democratization of the whole system.

It has often been suggested in the West that the leaders of Solidarity went too far with their demands and actions. But Western observers rarely raised one extremely important question: Why did the program of the union undergo this radicalization? Some observers pointed to Polish "hurrah-romanticism" and to the inexperience of Solidarity's leaders as factors forcing the confrontation with the Polish authorities which the union could not hope to win. But, admitting all that, we must carefully assess the motives of the leaders of Solidarity. The union really wanted to improve the conditions of life in Poland and prevent the destruction of the Polish economy, but in order to accomplish this it would have to introduce free-market mechanisms and establish some institutional means of social control (i.e., control by the people) over the communist government. Otherwise, scarcely any progress in the union's program could be made.

It was a period typical of a diarchy. The government retained the means of political and military pressure. Yet the system of *nomenklatura*, which had hitherto sustained the party, crumbled and slipped from the party's control. The government controlled the mass media, but its propaganda was countered by the freely published and widely distributed pamphlets and newspapers of Solidarity. The union had considerable social authority, but lacked sufficient means to pressure the government. Strikes, until then the only form of persuasion, proved ineffective and only further deepened the deterioration of the Polish economy. Solidarity's leaders could not cope with the radical attitudes of many workers. The people were impatient. Rank-and-file members, growing radical, opposed additional inconclusive negotiations. Time was on the government's side; the workers would be the losers in any kind of "dialogue." Both the government and Solidarity put forward programs of reform, but neither program could be realized.

Throughout the negotiations, the danger of Soviet intervention was the dominant, though unspoken, factor. Both sides knew such intervention to be possible—however inconvenient for Moscow. The Soviet invasion of Afghanistan complicated matters for the Kremlin, and Soviet economic prospects might be dealt a serious setback by any action in Poland. Poland's economic distress, which compelled Solidarity to act, provided an additional check on the Soviet Union—which was reluctant to assume responsibility for paying Poland's debts.

Under these circumstances, Moscow predictably preferred to pressure the Polish government to deal decisively with Solidarity. Yet both Moscow and Warsaw required time to draw up a plan of action.

The leaders of the union soon realized the nature of the Kremlin's strategy: The Polish government, under Soviet pressure, only pretended to engage in a dialogue with Solidarity, even suggesting compromises which might satisfy workers' demands but which the government had no intention of ever honoring. It was a lesson which taught the leaders of the union that the Communist Party is never a real partner in any negotiations. It became quite clear that if Solidarity wanted to save the country from economic collapse, it had to take some strong actions to force reforms upon the government. For that reason Solidarity, which never aspired to the role of a political organization, was forced to take on all the antidemocratic mechanisms of the totalitarian state—the hierarchical party system, the unlimited power of the party, the monopoly control of the mass media, education and culture, the absence of free elections, the centrally planned economy, the use of terror, and the prevalence of censorship. The advanced phase of the crisis of communism in Poland demanded this kind of action. The "stage of awareness" had shattered all illusions as to the good will of the communist regime. The society was still not openly anticommunist, but it was quite aware that reforms must be forced on the government which continuously provoked Solidarity, trying to prove to foreign observers that Poland was tottering on the brink of disaster.

The government's accusations that the leaders of Solidarity wanted to seize power were patently ridiculous. Yet it would also be naive to expect that in these circumstances Solidarity could act solely as a trade union. This was the biggest dilemma facing its leaders. If Solidarity wanted to implement its program, it had to act as a nationwide movement, with the purpose of implementing basic social and economic reforms. This kind of organization was totally unacceptable to the Communist Party. The government, which had no intention of cooperating with another institution of the Polish people, left no other options open to the union. Solidarity had to oppose the policies of the Polish Communist Party or give up its program and disappoint the Polish people. It had to attack the whole system or cease to exist at all.

The first indication of a possible confrontation was the concentration of power. General Jaruzelski, appointed to the principal posts of the state, seemed perfectly chosen. On the one hand, he had Moscow's confidence; on the other, during the events in the summer of 1981, he presented himself as a man of compromise, a moderate politician promising that arms would never be used against Polish workers. Already Secretary of Defense, Jaruzelski took over the post of Prime Minister in February 1981; following the Party Congress, he also became First Secretary of the Central Committee in October. These facts suggested that some action against Solidarity was being prepared.

For the most part, this scheme was successful. Some union leaders did not believe that any armed action would be taken by the Polish government against an organization with so much popular support. Other leaders, Lech Walesa among them, did not dismiss the possibility of military repression; they spoke openly of the danger of confrontation between Solidarity and the government. Yet, without some hostile action by the government, union leaders could not cease bargaining and go underground; so they waited, hoping the government might understand that, in the long run, any action undertaken against the entire nation must end in failure.

The government's actions that followed the declaration of martial law on December 13, 1981, were well concerted. The Military Council of National Salvation had been shrewdly chosen for its tasks. When the junta was ready to strike, Solidarity leaders and their supporting intellectuals were taken from the union's ongoing conference at the Congress of Culture and interned. Local leaders of Solidarity and the more aggressive scholars and students were seized at their offices and apartments. The country's entire system of communications was forcibly interrupted to make links between factories impossible. During the first few weeks following the proclamation of martial law, the biggest centers of resistance in the coal mines and steel factories were overcome by well-armed militia units, accompanied by military forces. Regular troops were rarely used in direct action, for the government did not have complete confidence in them.

The Phase of Isolation

The events following December 13, 1981, are well known. The stage of growing social awareness had culminated with the imposition of martial law. The State Council's decrees of December 13 completed this lesson vital to the process of educating the Polish people. Martial law, which restrained the activity of Solidarity, brought the Communist Party, for the first time, face to face with the general populace—which not only expressed opposition to party policy, but openly manifested anticommunist attitudes.

The imposition of martial law also marked the beginning of the next period of the crisis: the stage of the Communist Party's isolation from society. Even old communists, disappointed in Jaruzelski's policy, expressed opposition. The many resignations of party members deprived the Polish Communist Party of its (relatively) better elements.

Although the government succeeded, it was not easy to measure the degree of its success. Certainly it was easier to win than to retain the advantages of victory. Those Solidarity members who evaded imprisonment went underground, but their activities became increasingly perceptible. The demonstrations at the beginning of 1982 proved that the union still had nationwide support; the union's ideas have remained popular; and Lech Walesa, widely recognized as a charismatic personality, became a national hero. Solidarity was suspended—but it still existed and functioned; and the junta, after imposing martial law, was fully aware of the union's social power.

The Church, following a wait-and-see policy for a few weeks, stiffened its attitude and began to criticize the policies of the Military Council more openly. Local clergy began to support underground attempts to restore the union's activities. The Catholic hierarchy tried to mediate between the union and the government, but the developing subjugation of the Polish economy to that of the Soviet Union undercut these efforts. The Catholic Church, traditionally sensitive to Poland's relationship with the Soviet Union, felt its social position imperiled and feared that a tighter control by Moscow over the Policy economy might be followed by an anti-religious policy typical of the Stalinist period.

Nor did the junta anticipate the reaction of the West: Economic sanctions infuriated the communist government and mass media, which promptly

stepped up its propaganda line proclaiming the new regime a great success—
a technique previously used during the Gomulka and Gierek regimes.

Military government, suitable only for a state of emergency, soon showed
itself ineffectual in the face of grave economic, social, and international
problems. The more profound the difficulties of a state, the more acute the
problems become under military rule. The longer a military regime endures,
the more its officers find it necessary to compromise with important elements
in society.

This was the situation in Poland in 1982. Without cooperation from the
West, Poland's economic troubles could not be alleviated. Polish industry
was almost wholly dependent on Western raw materials, spare parts, and
foreign technology. This dependence was caused by the blunders of the
Gierek government which, having at its disposal considerable amounts of
foreign currency derived from unrestricted Western loans, decided to import
as much as possible in an effort to accelerate the industrialization of Poland.
It was obvious that, under these circumstances, if the West maintained its
tough stance and continued its economic sanctions, Poland would not be
able to surmount its difficulties without help from other foreign sources.
With the Polish population engaged in passive resistance and deliberate
work slowdowns, the junta could not rely on continued assistance from
Moscow. The Soviet Union, with its own economic problems, could not feed
the Poles for any great length of time. Scarcities of raw materials and spare
parts began to cause lengthy standstills in factories. Unemployment, swelling
inflation, and severe food shortages could produce fierce social unrest in
the near future. The junta realized that if the West held to its course of
economic sanctions and the Poles continued to resist the military regime,
the collapse—the total collapse—of the Polish economy was inevitable. The
military government needed a program which could bring the country out
of this dangerous impasse.

Finally the totalitarian or neo-Stalinist scheme supported by the hardliners
from the party machinery gained the upper hand. It resulted from a
realization of the isolation of the party. Its proponents recognized that only
uncompromising terror could rule a society that had become aware of the
deficiencies of communism. This scheme involved establishing one trade
union, completely purged of all dissenters, and advocated the extermination
of all opposition and the reintegration of the Polish economy with the Soviet
central planning apparatus. It provided essentially for a program of semi-
colonial dependence on the Soviet Union: the substantial part of Polish
industry was to utilize Soviet raw materials, process them, and send finished
products to the East.

The dissolution of Solidarity on October 9, 1982, by the communist-
dominated parliament was to signify the adoption of this scheme. This
policy has placed the members of this once powerful union in a difficult

and dangerous situation and has driven home to most of its members that few of Solidarity's objectives will be realized—at least in the foreseeable future.

Solidarity's strategy of wearing down the government through passive resistance had been effective only to a limited degree. It showed that the government could not cope with continuing demonstrations, strikes, and other manifestations of public discontent—without taking the sternest measures under martial law. Yet, Solidarity's strategy had not succeeded in pushing the military junta toward compromise.

Solidarity's leaders could have ignored the decisions of the Polish parliament at their own peril and proceeded along their previous course, but they had become aware that their hope of compelling a compromise had been shattered.

For the junta, it was quite obvious that the decision to dissolve Solidarity would provoke a spontaneous reaction among the workers. The military government, expecting a confrontation with the opposition, was prepared for bloody repression.

The junta's expectations were correct. However, the strikes and demonstrations following the formal liquidation of Solidarity were uncoordinated, and the leaders of the underground movement themselves tried to restrain the workers, in part because the outlawed union wanted to choose its own moment for the next confrontation. Solidarity leaders decided that a four-hour nationwide work stoppage on November 10 would be a proper test of the power of the union. Yet, after the event, even the underground Polish press acknowledged that this attempt to hold a limited general strike was a failure. The workers did not want to risk their lives and jobs in another show of power. The underground union found itself in a very difficult situation. Union leaders did not want to give up, but they could not promise the workers ultimate victory. In the view of some leaders, only permanent opposition and repeated strikes and demonstrations would convince the Soviet Union that the Polish junta had erred in outlawing Solidarity, and that only real concessions could restore order in Poland. In the long run this appraisal of the situation may prove to have been correct. But for workers exhausted by two-and-a-half years of unceasing struggles, the argument was not convincing.

Soon after the outlawing of Solidarity the junta officially approved plans for a visit by the Pope to Poland in June 1983, but announced that the project depended on the situation in Poland. This clever ploy provided an additional incentive for workers not to participate in strikes and demonstrations, for they did not want to be blamed for a delay in the Pope's visit to Poland.

Leonid Brezhnev's death might have provoked a renewal of tension in Poland. The junta realized that this event strengthened the position of the militants in Solidarity. The radicals could point out, not without reason, that the uncertainty in Soviet policy following the change in leadership would be conducive to the success of general strikes or nationwide uprising. It would be highly inconvenient for the Polish government if the new Soviet leaders perceived that Warsaw still could not cope with the situation. These calculations probably resulted in the junta's decision to release Lech Walesa, a decision that for the short term eased the situation in Poland.

The government again guessed correctly. Several factors contributed to the relatively quiet reception of changes in the Soviet leadership: the unsuccessful strikes earlier in November in Poland, the quick appointment of Yuri Andropov, and Walesa's release. But most important was the union's failure to devise new tactics following the dissolution of Solidarity.

Lessons from the Polish Crisis

Events in Poland since mid-1980 have provided illuminating lessons for observers of communist politics—lessons not only for the Poles but for all who underestimated the crisis of communism in Eastern Europe.

Many commentaries on the history of independent Polish unions have asked: Why could the relatively easy "victory" gained in 1980 not be repeated after the imposition of martial law? In December 1981, Solidarity was stronger and more aware of its power; it could boast of the support of the majority of the nation. Why then did the attempted general strike fail in December 1981?

Even if we agree that Solidarity was pushed to confrontation and provoked by the government, we must admit that the union's leaders underestimated the most obvious and powerful mechanisms of the communist system. The great majority of union members erroneously calculated that "power lies in the streets." They mistook economic leverage for military power and did not anticipate that a government unable to deal with economic problems would nonetheless be in a position to suppress a whole people fighting for freedom. The communists may not know much about how to govern, but they know a lot about how to seize and hang on to power. Overestimating the spontaneity of the movement in August 1980, union leaders did not attach enough importance to objective phenomena favoring the movement in the moment of its emergence. Solidarity's leaders did not realize the simple truth that all victories result in equal measure from the strength of the victors and the weakness of the defeated. The crisis of communism enfeebled the machinery of totalitarian control, but it did not destroy it totally. Without a proper understanding of the difference between a collapse and a crisis of communism, no opposition can be a match for a totalitarian regime.

The lessons of winter 1981 and the next ten months were not lost on the Polish communists. Those events demonstrated that the communist government could not gain the support of either the Church or the general population—unless it compromised on several important matters, which it was not prepared to do. Without support from either Church or populace, the government could not deal adequately with urgent social problems.

The remaining Communist Party cadres have begun to recognize that no measures they can take will compensate for the losses suffered in the battle with Solidarity. It has become increasingly clear that the party lost the confidence of the general public forever and with it the possibility of manipulating the public's social attitudes. Prospects for restoring intermediate structures between the government and the general public are bleak. The public cannot be induced to believe again that the distortions of communist practice are temporary; Poles now generally perceive that these distortions are permanently rooted in the communist system.

Poland's Communist Party has begun to realize, too, that its method of shifting and rehabilitating party elites by the elevation of a new charismatic leader is not effective. New Party cadres seem to lose their credibility forever.

Most significant, however, was the failure of the economic program of the neo-Stalinist hardliners. The attempt at quick insertion of a substantial part of Polish industry into the Soviet central planning system proved to be infeasible. Polish factories working with Western technologies cannot easily process Soviet raw materials and adapt spare parts that are not of Western design.

The Polish junta found itself caught between four conflicting forces: the nearly complete collapse of the Polish economy; the pressure of the Soviet Union, which expected positive results more quickly from the military "coup d'etat"; the crippling Western economic sanctions; and the continued resistance of the underground Solidarity movement and Polish society. In 1980-1981, the Polish government seemed to have a lot of time to defend its position. Solidarity, a new factor in Polish social life, had to prove that it could carry out an effective program. After the dissolution of Solidarity, the junta, responsible for everything and under Soviet control, had to move fast. For that reason, the military government of General Jaruzelski, isolated from society and deprived of all supporting structures, began eagerly to seek allies. The Catholic Church—the third (next to the Communist Party and Solidarity) most significant power in Poland—became the target of a moderate flirtation from the junta, which finally resulted in Jaruzelski's decision to permit the Polish Pope to visit his homeland. The Polish crisis confirmed something that had never been questioned—the military potential of the system. Yet it also revealed the vulnerability of communism. It proved that the internal crisis is a fact, that the protest of the once isolated intellectuals has become transformed into a nationwide anticommunist front.

A future crisis in Poland, similar to the turbulence of 1980-1981, might undermine even the loyalty of the army to the regime. Western observers often remarked that Solidarity did not gain the support of the Polish soldiers. To understand why this happened, we must realize that the soldiers of the 1978 and 1979 drafts had been in the army almost three years, since their military service had been prolonged by the government. Subjected to unceasing communist propaganda, they received almost all their information concerning Solidarity from party sources. Even if they sympathized with the union, they did not experience the special atmosphere in which the movement was born because they did not participate in the meetings, strikes, and street demonstrations. But these young men cannot be kept as troops forever. The next several drafts must bring into the army a generation composed of recent members of Solidarity, who are familiar with the goals of the union, who may have participated in the struggle against the government. This prospect must worry new party leaders because it could shift the balance of power decisively against the Communist Party in an eventual confrontation. The series of uprisings of the Polish type might significantly affect even the Soviet military establishment.

The opponents of the thesis that communism is in crisis repeatedly argue that the Soviet system has survived many crises including counterrevolution, the period of the New Economic Policy, Stalin's nationalization and collectivization campaigns, famine in the Ukraine (when people were dying of starvation at the rate of 25,000 a day[112]), the purges of the 1930s, World War II, and other upheavals. They see no evidence that it will not be able to handle the current problems as well.

In my opinion, communism has in reality passed through only several stages of the same crisis. The recent one in Poland added a new component to the previous defects of the system: the growing awareness of the crisis. It is far more serious than the ideological perplexities which troubled the revisionists of the 1950s or 1960s. They either criticized the system as departing from orthodox Marxism or believed that they would be able to design a model of communism compatible with current needs. But now, doubts about the genuine communist character of the Soviet model have gradually been replaced by the conviction that this model (whether it is communist or not) has no future. The Soviet system is now widely viewed as a trap in which the societies of the bloc have been caught. This trap can be crushed from outside, blown out from inside, or simply smashed to pieces

---

[112] See James E. Mace, "The Man-Made Famine of 1933 in the Soviet Ukraine: What Happened and Why?," paper delivered at the International Conference on the Holocaust and Genocide, in Tel Aviv, Israel, June 20-24, 1982; James E. Mace, "Soviets still hide their dark deeds in Ukraine," *The Record*, September 4, 1984; Bohdan Krawchenko, "The Great Famine of 1932-33 in the Soviet Ukraine," *One World*, Spring 1989; Timothy Quinlow, "The Great Ukrainian Hunger Holocaust, 1932-33," *New York City Tribune*, June 17, 1985.

through outside and inside pressure, but the model cannot be transformed into a safe shelter which can offer protection and prosperity for its inhabitants. This consciousness separates those who still protect the framework of the trap and those who are imprisoned inside. It results in the dwindling not only of the group of real believers in communism, but also of the group of reliable party bureaucrats who were cynical before, but still believed that the system would secure them, their children, and grandchildren a successful future, even if it had to be achieved at the expense of the masses. This belief has been severely undermined by the awareness of the crisis which is now gradually reaching the consciousness of the party bureaucrats. The Polish crisis showed that party functionaries feel endangered by the social ostracism and isolation that they are experiencing. The party might test new strategies and try to establish new intermediate social structures, but it is most unlikely that the communist system will be able to curb the process of awakening that is affecting all groups and all nations of the Soviet bloc.

5.
Conclusions

WILL THE CRISIS of communism be localized in Poland or will it spread, step by step, to the other countries of the Soviet bloc? There are already some developments which hint at an answer to this question. Realistically, there is little likelihood of the diffusion of the Polish "disease." It would be too optimistic to believe that the Polish ferment will automatically infect other societies of East Central Europe. Alex Pravda summarized it best: "Since there seems to be some misunderstanding on this point in the West, it is worth noting that there never was any serious prospect of a Solidarity-type movement emerging elsewhere in Eastern Europe, let alone in the Soviet Union. The phenomenon of 1980-1981 was the result of a particular combination of circumstances. . . . "[113] The national character of the Polish people is responsible for the fact that many aspects of Solidarity are unique to Poland. Of course, there have been some signs of support for the Polish struggle. A small group of Czech dissidents sent a letter of support to Polish workers who struck in Gdansk, and some workers in Moscow were favorably disposed toward the Polish independent trade union. These responses should not be underestimated, but they cannot be regarded as significant attempts to follow in Solidarity's footsteps.

Western observers have questioned whether the working class in other socialist countries is mature enough to create a Solidarity-type political movement. They have noted that totalitarian regimes are often successful in attempts to atomize their societies and encourage self-centered attitudes rather than a spirit of unity and civic cooperation. The assessment by Andrei Amalrik of some attributes of the Russian national character has often been quoted in Western literature:

In general, when the average Russian sees that he is living less well than his neighbour, he will concentrate not on trying to do better for himself but rather on trying to bring his neighbour down to his own level. My reasoning may seem naive to some people, but I have been able to observe sources of examples in both village and town, and I see in this one of the typical traits of the Russian psyche.[114]

---

[113] Alex Pravda, "Solidarity and the Soviet Bloc: A Workers Under Communism Symposium," *Workers Under Communism*, Fall 1982, No. 2.

[114] Amalrik, *Will the Soviet Union Survive Until 1984?*, op. cit., p. 35.

The tendency to find someone else's success more painful than his own failure is not typical of only the Russian people. It is a sort of communist psychological syndrome which for decades has worked against anticommunist unity among people in various socialist countries. This tendency is shrewdly encouraged by Soviet propaganda, which has spread rumors that, for example, Poland is in economic depression because it has had to subsidize Cuba, India, and other international communist adventures; or that the Czech and Hungarian economies have deteriorated because of assistance given to the Poles who are "lazy and simply do not want to work." Thanks to this psychological syndrome, such stories are often welcome in "brother socialist countries."

The fact that there is little chance that the other countries of the Soviet bloc will promptly follow the lead of Polish Solidarity does not mean, however, that the crisis of communism will be localized in Poland. The next stages of the crisis of the whole system are not dependent upon the spread of this particular Polish virus. Nor do they require the sympathy of other oppressed peoples for the Poles or Polish political culture. These next stages, rather, depend on a duplication of the Polish experience in another Soviet bloc country, where similar political, economic, and social objectives emerge. Sooner or later the workers in other socialist countries will themselves replicate the Polish experience. It would be too optimistic to believe that the Polish ferment will automatically infect other societies of East Central Europe. The process of maturation may take time but the potential for the rise of a free workers' movement exists in each socialist country.[115] Similar ideological, economic, and social unrest can drive the countries of the Soviet bloc in the same direction. The Polish crisis may not spread, but the Polish experience might be roughly duplicated in a fashion that will accord with the national characteristics of other countries in the Eastern bloc. As Daniel Singer wrote:

Poland, having shown the way, needs not necessarily remain in the lead. Each country and each movement have their handicaps and their assets. East Germany, burdened with Prussian discipline, also has a true Marxist tradition, illustrated by people like Rudolf Bahro. Czechoslovakia, while strangled by the most repressive system, has not only its Chartists; it also has the collective memory of the Prague Spring and the admittedly ambiguous feeling that a popular movement might have changed the shape of the future. In Hungary, nearly a quarter of a century after the event, the bloody invasion still preys on the national consciousness. On the other hand, it is in Hungary that the economic experiment has gone further and may soon begin to loosen the social fabric. Finally, the Soviet Union itself combines the most ruthless and rigid mechanisms of power with a very acute economic dilemma and, possibly, the most explosive potential.[116]

---

[115] See Albert Shanker, "Solidarity and the Soviet Bloc," *Workers Under Communism*, Fall 1982, No. 2, p. 11.

[116] Singer, *The Road to Gdansk*, op. cit., p. 194.

There are already some indications that the "process of maturation" might not take very long. The economic, ideological, moral, financial, and social crisis has affected all centrally-planned economies. Parallels between the other countries of the Soviet bloc and Poland are obvious. The societies of these countries are also in conflict with their communist authorities, yet they are not ready to protest militantly against their totalitarian regimes. The stagnant economies of these countries are incapable of producing enough consumer goods and meeting workers' demands which will increase with the growth of education and consumerism. Workers in other countries of the bloc will not expect less than the Poles. Furthermore, tensions in Eastern Europe are likely to become more acute in the future, as the gap in the standard of living between the countries of the Soviet bloc and the West increases.

It is unquestionable that consumer demand is becoming a greater problem even in the Soviet Union. The Soviet leaders realize that a repeated application of Stalinist methods to suppress the trend toward consumerism might not be successful this time. As Seweryn Bialer pointed out:

The growth of Soviet consumption in the Brezhnev era, 1965-80, can be evaluated as constituting 4.6 percent yearly and the growth of per capita consumption as being 3.4 percent yearly. The baseline projection for the 1981-5 period envisaged a consumption growth of 2.1 percent and per capita consumption growth of 1.2 percent, that is, a growth already less than half of the preceding fifteen years in total consumption and only a little over one-third in the per capita consumption growth. If further inroads were to be made into these very modest projected figures by reallocation away from consumption, then for all practical purposes the standard of living of the Soviet population would freeze at the present level or might even decline.[117]

It is not true that Soviet leaders are unconcerned with the standard of living of the Soviet people. On the contrary, consumerism was viewed in the Brezhnev era as a way of gaining popular acceptance for the regime, and Soviet leaders realize that lack of success in dealing with economic problems may increase the gap between the rulers and the ruled—may lead to a further decline of faith in the promises of a better life under communism and to a new wave of citizen discontent.

A trend toward consumerism is particularly strong in Czechoslovakia and Hungary. The economies of these countries, although they leave much to be desired, have not been affected by a crisis as serious as the Polish economic collapse. Yet even in these countries, the real wages of workers have fallen because of inflation. The authorities will obviously try to make some concessions and maintain the illusion that the influence of state-controlled unions

---

[117] Bialer, *Stalin's Successors*, op. cit., p. 293.

is growing, but their actions will not prevent deterioration of economic conditions even in these countries. The growth of savings-bank accounts is a sign of growing inflation. Shortages of most basic commodities are widespread and store shelves are frequently empty.

One cannot reliably anticipate which of the bloc countries might be the first to follow Poland's example. There are, however, some indications that after a period of political apathy, the second half of the 1980s will witness some dissidence in Czechoslovakia. The Charter movement of 1977 showed that the atmosphere of social unrest that led to the "Prague Spring" in 1968 did not wither away completely; the dissident movement merely changed its character. According to Z.L. Suda,

> the ferment, which, during the liberalization era and in the preceding years, took place in the center of the party or close to it, has now shifted to a gray zone on the periphery of power, where rank-and-file party members, party-sponsored groups, and unorganized public opinion blend into one. While the nonconformism of the 1960s was propagated by a triple alliance of intellectuals, economists, and young party apparatchiks, with the unaffiliated public waiting and showing various degrees of interest, the activists of the late 1970s and the early 1980s have been recruited from both camps.[118]

Czech nonconformism today is not as elitist and spectacular as in 1968, but its popular background allows one to view the maturation of Czech dissidents with some optimism. Political commentators point to a radicalization rather than to a moderation of the Czech dissident movement, which seems to view the struggle for human rights as only a first step toward transformation in all spheres of social and economic life.

> They call for pluralism, without the crippling qualifications characteristic of the Action Program of April 1968. This implies the rejection of the "leading role of the party"—a rejection that comes easily since the preservation of the alleged "accomplishments of socialism" (a lofty term for the state-owned and bureaucratically operated economy) is no longer the number-one priority. Having taken this step, the nonconformists have freed themselves from the need to "square the circle" faced by the protagonists of the Prague Spring; namely, the establishment of a pluralist society within a one-party state.[119]

Protests and strikes have also been observed in the Soviet Union. They occurred in Riga in May 1976; in Kostamuksha near Finland in February 1979; in Abkhazia in April and October 1978; and in Baku in January 1979.[120] In 1980 and 1981, strikes were reported in many places throughout the Soviet Union but were given little publicity by the Soviet media.

---

[118] Z.L. Suda, "Czechoslovakia: An Aborted Reform," in Drachkovitch, editor, *East Central Europe* . . . , op. cit., p. 255.

[119] Ibid., p. 257.

[120] See Goldman, *USSR in Crisis* . . . , op. cit., p. xi.

The "stage of awareness" in the Soviet Union awaits the re-education of Russian society, the development of a new individualistic mentality. It is a natural process of socio-psychological recovery, following centuries of authoritarian and totalitarian terror. Yet, this process, once the inertia of centuries is overcome, could unfold with amazing rapidity. The results might be sporadic and immature in the beginning, but the movement against the "collective mentality" promoted by the regime might be very strong and in the long run irresistible. Even the traditional patient endurance of the Soviet population has its limits. A Russian proverb says that "the naked fear no bandit." The Russian populace is more and more aware that this proverb is a perfect analogy to its situation. The West really underestimates the rise of popular expectations in the Soviet bloc and still tends to view Russian citizens only as people who are resilient and long-suffering. "But for how long can this continue?," ask Arnold Beichman and Mikhail S. Bernstam in their excellent book on Andropov. "Ruthlessness and repression alone cannot solve the Soviet Union's economic, demographic, and political problems. There are indications that the Soviet people are not as easily intimidated as they were in the 1930s and the postwar 1950s."[121] The future might prove that there is much more potential for violence in the Russian masses than is generally attributed to them. Until recently this potential was dampened by an illusion of the temporary character of the crisis. The growing awareness of the irreversible failure of the system to respond to popular demands may result in serious domestic ferment.

My remarks on the crisis of communism have often been questioned on the grounds that they are based on unjustified optimism. I do not deny my optimism, but this has nothing to do with my real intentions. The purpose of this study is not to generate predictions and prophecies. An historian may attempt to anticipate forthcoming events, but by the nature of things he will always have incomplete knowledge of all the factors that might contribute to the future. My purpose has been to point out the main factors that may contribute to the final corrosion of the totalitarian system, but such a development will depend as much on internal developments in the Soviet bloc as on the attitudes of the Western countries—which often seem unaware that the crisis of communism is also their problem.

The West must be alert to the crisis wherever it arises, but must also not ignore the fact that while Soviet communism is decaying internally, it can grow in influence externally. The future of communism depends not only on whether turbulence returns to Poland and other countries of the Soviet bloc, but also on whether the West finally learns that the idea of solidarity is more than a Polish curiosity.

---

[121] Beichman and Bernstam, *Andropov . . .* , op. cit., p. 207.

PERGAMON-BRASSEY'S
International Defense Publishers

List of Publications
published for the
Institute for Foreign Policy Analysis, Inc.

Orders for the following titles should be addressed to: Pergamon-Brassey's, Maxwell House, Fairview Park, Elmsford, New York, 10523; or to Pergamon-Brassey's, Headington Hill Hall, Oxford, OX3 0BW, England.

Foreign Policy Reports

ETHICS,DETERRENCE, AND NATIONAL SECURITY. By James E. Dougherty, Midge Decter, Pierre Hassner, Laurence Martin, Michael Novak, and Vladimir Bukovsky. June 1985. xvi, 91pp. $9.95.

AMERICAN SEA POWER AND GLOBAL STRATEGY. By Robert J. Hanks. October 1985. viii, 92pp. $9.95.

DECISION-MAKING IN COMMUNIST COUNTRIES: AN INSIDE VIEW. By Jan Sejna and Joseph D. Douglass, Jr. 1986. xii, 75pp. $9.95.

NATIONAL SECURITY: ETHICS, STRATEGY, AND POLITICS. A LAYMAN'S PRIMER. By Robert L. Pfaltzgraff, Jr. 1986.v, 37pp. $9.95.

DETERRING CHEMICAL WARFARE: U.S. POLICY OPTIONS FOR THE 1990S. By Hugh Stringer. 1986. xii, 71pp. $9.95.

Special Reports

STRATEGIC MINERALS AND INTERNATIONAL SECURITY. Edited by Uri Ra'anan and Charles M. Perry. July 1985. viii, 85pp. $9.95.

THIRD WORLD MARXIST-LENINIST REGIMES: STRENGTHS, VULNERABILITIES, AND U.S. POLICY. By Uri Ra'anan, Francis Fukuyama, Mark Falcoff, Sam C. Sarkesian, and Richard H. Shultz, Jr. September 1985. xv, 125pp. $9.95.

THE RED ARMY ON PAKISTAN'S BORDER: POLICY IMPLICATIONS FOR THE UNITED STATES. By Anthony Arnold, Richard P. Cronin, Thomas Perry Thornton, Theodore L. Eliot, Jr., and Robert L. Pfaltzgraff, Jr. 1986. vi, 82pp. $9.95.

Books

ATLANTIC COMMUNITY IN CRISIS: A REDEFINITION OF THE ATLANTIC RELATIONSHIP. Edited by Walter F. Hahn and Robert L. Pfaltzgraff, Jr. 1979. 386pp. $43.00.

REVISING U.S. MILITARY STRATEGY: TAILORING MEANS TO ENDS. By Jeffrey Record. 1984. 113pp. $16.95 ($9.95, paper).

SHATTERING EUROPE'S DEFENSE CONSENSUS: THE ANTINUCLEAR PROTEST MOVEMENT AND THE FUTURE OF NATO. Edited by James E. Dougherty and Robert L. Pfaltzgraff, Jr. 1985. 226pp. $18.95.

INSTITUTE FOR FOREIGN POLICY ANALYSIS, INC.
List of Publications

Orders for the following titles in IFPA's series of Special Reports, Foreign Policy Reports, National Security Papers, Conference Reports, and Books should be addressed to the Circulation Manager, Institute for Foreign Policy Analysis, Central Plaza Building, Tenth Floor, 675 Massachusetts Avenue, Cambridge, Massachusetts 02139-3396. (Telephone: 617-492-2116.) Please send a check or money order for the correct amount together with your order.

Foreign Policy Reports

DEFENSE TECHNOLOGY AND THE ATLANTIC ALLIANCE: COMPETITION OR COLLABORATION? By Frank T.J. Bray and Michael Moodie. April 1977. vi, 42pp. $5.00.

IRAN'S QUEST FOR SECURITY: U.S. ARMS TRANSFERS AND THE NUCLEAR OPTION. By Alvin J. Cottrell and James E. Dougherty. May 1977. 59pp. $5.00.

ETHIOPIA, THE HORN OF AFRICA, AND U.S. POLICY. By John H. Spencer. September 1977. 69pp. $5.00.

BEYOND THE ARAB-ISRAELI SETTLEMENT: NEW DIRECTIONS FOR U.S. POLICY IN THE MIDDLE EAST. By R.K. Ramazani. September 1977. viii, 69pp. $5.00.

SPAIN, THE MONARCHY AND THE ATLANTIC COMMUNITY. By David C. Jordan. June 1979. v, 55pp. $5.00.

U.S. STRATEGY AT THE CROSSROADS: TWO VIEWS. By Robert J. Hanks and Jeffrey Record. July 1982. viii, 69pp. $7.50.

THE U.S. MILITARY PRESENCE IN THE MIDDLE EAST: PROBLEMS AND PROSPECTS. By Robert J. Hanks. December 1982. vii, 77pp. $7.50.

SOUTHERN AFRICA AND WESTERN SECURITY. By Robert J. Hanks. August 1983. vii, 71pp. $7.50.

THE WEST GERMAN PEACE MOVEMENT AND THE NATIONAL QUESTION. By Kim R. Holmes. March 1984. x, 73pp. $7.50.

THE HISTORY AND IMPACT OF MARXIST-LENINIST ORGANIZATIONAL THEORY. By John P. Roche. April 1984. x, 70pp. $7.50.

Special Reports

THE CRUISE MISSILE: BARGAINING CHIP OR DEFENSE BARGAIN? By Robert L. Pfaltzgraff, Jr., and Jacquelyn K. Davis. January 1977. x, 53pp. $3.00.

EUROCOMMUNISM AND THE ATLANTIC ALLIANCE. By James E. Dougherty and Diane K. Pfaltzgraff. January 1977. xiv, 66pp. $3.00.

THE NEUTRON BOMB: POLITICAL, TECHNICAL, AND MILITARY ISSUES. By S.T. Cohen. November 1978. xii, 95pp. $6.50.

SALT II AND U.S.-SOVIET STRATEGIC FORCES. By Jacquelyn K. Davis, Patrick J. Friel, and Robert L. Pfaltzgraff, Jr. June 1979. xii, 51pp. $5.00.

THE EMERGING STRATEGIC ENVIRONMENT: IMPLICATIONS FOR BALLISTIC MISSILE DEFENSE. By Leon Gouré, William G. Hyland, and Colin S. Gray. December 1979. xi, 75pp. $6.50.

THE SOVIET UNION AND BALLISTIC MISSILE DEFENSE. By Jacquelyn K. Davis, Uri Ra'anan, Robert L. Pfaltzgraff, Jr., Michael J. Deane, and John M. Collins. March 1980. xi, 71pp. $6.50. (Out of print).

ENERGY ISSUES AND ALLIANCE RELATIONSHIPS: THE UNITED STATES, WESTERN EUROPE AND JAPAN. By Robert L. Pfaltzgraff, Jr. April 1980. xii, 71pp. $6.50.

U.S. STRATEGIC-NUCLEAR POLICY AND BALLISTIC MISSILE DEFENSE: THE 1980S AND BEYOND. By William Schneider, Jr., Donald G. Brennan, William A. Davis, Jr., and Hans Rühle. April 1980. xii, 61pp. $6.50.

THE UNNOTICED CHALLENGE: SOVIET MARITIME STRATEGY AND THE GLOBAL CHOKE POINTS. By Robert J. Hanks. August 1980. xi, 66pp. $6.50.

FORCE REDUCTIONS IN EUROPE: STARTING OVER. By Jeffrey Record. October 1980. xi, 91pp. $6.50.

SALT II AND AMERICAN SECURITY. By Gordon J. Humphrey, William R. Van Cleave, Jeffrey Record, William H. Kincade, and Richard Perle. October 1980. xvi, 65pp.

THE FUTURE OF U.S. LAND-BASED STRATEGIC FORCES. By Jake Garn, J.I. Coffey, Lord Chalfont, and Ellery B. Block. December 1980. xvi, 80pp.

THE CAPE ROUTE: IMPERILED WESTERN LIFELINE. By Robert J. Hanks. February 1981. xi, 80pp. $6.50. (Hardcover, $10.00).

POWER PROJECTION AND THE LONG-RANGE COMBAT AIRCRAFT: MISSIONS, CAPABILITIES AND ALTERNATIVE DESIGNS. By Jacquelyn K. Davis and Robert L. Pfaltzgraff, Jr. June 1981. ix, 37pp. $6.50.

THE PACIFIC FAR EAST: ENDANGERED AMERICAN STRATEGIC POSITION. By Robert J. Hanks. October 1981. vii, 75pp. $7.50.

NATO'S THEATER NUCLEAR FORCE MODERNIZATION PROGRAM: THE REAL ISSUES. By Jeffrey Record. November 1981. viii, 102pp. $7.50.

THE CHEMISTRY OF DEFEAT: ASYMMETRIES IN U.S. AND SOVIET CHEMICAL WARFARE POSTURES. By Amoretta M. Hoeber. December 1981. xiii, 91pp. $6.50.

THE HORN OF AFRICA: A MAP OF POLITICAL-STRATEGIC CONFLICT. By James E. Dougherty. April 1982. xv, 74pp. $7.50.

THE WEST, JAPAN AND CAPE ROUTE IMPORTS: THE OIL AND NON-FUEL MINERAL TRADES. By Charles Perry. June 1982. xiv, 88pp. $7.50.

THE RAPID DEPLOYMENT FORCE AND U.S. MILITARY INTERVENTION IN THE PERSIAN GULF. By Jeffrey Record. May 1983, Second Edition. viii, 83pp. $7.50.

THE GREENS OF WEST GERMANY: ORIGINS, STRATEGIES, AND TRANSATLANTIC IMPLICATIONS. By Robert L. Pfaltzgraff, Jr., Kim R. Holmes, Clay Clemens, and Werner Kaltefleiter. August 1983. xi, 105pp. $7.50.

THE ATLANTIC ALLIANCE AND U.S. GLOBAL STRATEGY. By Jacquelyn K. Davis and Robert L. Pfaltzgraff, Jr. September 1983. x, 44pp. $7.50.

WORLD ENERGY SUPPLY AND INTERNATIONAL SECURITY. By Herman Franssen, John P. Hardt, Jacquelyn K. Davis, Robert J. Hanks, Charles Perry, Robert L. Pfaltzgraff, Jr., and Jeffrey Record. October 1983. xiv, 93pp. $7.50.

POISONING ARMS CONTROL: THE SOVIET UNION AND CHEMICAL/BIOLOGICAL WEAPONS. By Mark C. Storella. June 1984. xi, 99pp. $7.50.

National Security Papers

CBW: THE POOR MAN'S ATOMIC BOMB. By Neil C. Livingstone and Joseph D. Douglass, Jr., with a Foreword by Senator John Tower. February 1984. x, 33pp. $5.00.

U.S. STRATEGIC AIRLIFT: REQUIREMENTS AND CAPABILITIES. By Jeffrey Record. January 1986. vi, 38pp. $6.00.

STRATEGIC BOMBERS: HOW MANY ARE ENOUGH? By Jeffrey Record. January 1986. vi, 22pp. $6.00.

STRATEGIC DEFENSE AND EXTENDED DETERRENCE: A NEW TRANSATLANTIC DEBATE. By Jacquelyn K. Davis and Robert L. Pfaltzgraff, Jr. February 1986. viii, 53pp. $8.00.

JCS REORGANIZATION AND U.S. ARMS CONTROL POLICY. By James E. Dougherty. March 1986. xiv, 27pp. $6.00.

STRATEGIC FORCE MODERNIZATION AND ARMS CONTROL. Contributions by Edward L. Rowny, R. James Woolsey, Harold Brown, Alexander M. Haig, Jr., Albert Gore, Jr., Brent Scowcroft, Russell E. Dougherty, A. Casey, Gordon Fornell, and Sam Nunn. 1986. xi, 43pp. $6.00.

Books

SOVIET MILITARY STRATEGY IN EUROPE. By Joseph D. Douglass, Jr. Pergamon Press, 1980. 252pp. (Out of print).

THE WARSAW PACT: ARMS, DOCTRINE, AND STRATEGY. By William J. Lewis. New York: McGraw-Hill Publishing Co., 1982. 471pp. $15.00.

THE BISHOPS AND NUCLEAR WEAPONS: THE CATHOLIC PASTORAL LETTER ON WAR AND PEACE. By James E. Dougherty. Archon Books, 1984. 255pp. $22.50.

Conference Reports

NATO AND ITS FUTURE: A GERMAN-AMERICAN ROUNDTABLE. Summary of a Dialogue. 1978. 22pp. $1.00.

SECOND GERMAN-AMERICAN ROUNDTABLE ON NATO: THE THEATER-NUCLEAR BALANCE. 1978. 32pp. $1.00.

THE SOVIET UNION AND BALLISTIC MISSILE DEFENSE. 1978. 26pp. $1.00.

U.S. STRATEGIC-NUCLEAR POLICY AND BALLISTIC MISSILE DEFENSE: THE 1980S AND BEYOND. 1979. 30pp. $1.00.

SALT II AND AMERICAN SECURITY. 1979. 39pp.

THE FUTURE OF U.S. LAND-BASED STRATEGIC FORCES. 1979. 32pp.

THE FUTURE OF NUCLEAR POWER. 1980. 48pp. $1.00.

THIRD GERMAN-AMERICAN ROUNDTABLE ON NATO: MUTUAL AND BALANCED FORCE REDUCTIONS IN EUROPE. 1980. 27pp. $1.00.

FOURTH GERMAN-AMERICAN ROUNDTABLE ON NATO: NATO MODERNIZATION AND EUROPEAN SECURITY. 1981. 15pp. $1.00.

SECOND ANGLO-AMERICAN SYMPOSIUM ON DETERRENCE AND EUROPEAN SECURITY. 1981. 25pp. $1.00.

THE U.S. DEFENSE MOBILIZATION INFRASTRUCTURE: PROBLEMS AND PRIORITIES. The Tenth Annual Conference, sponsored by the International Security Studies Program, The Fletcher School of Law and Diplomacy, Tufts University. 1981. 25pp. $1.00.

U.S. STRATEGIC DOCTRINE FOR THE 1980S. 1982. 14pp.

FRENCH-AMERICAN SYMPOSIUM ON STRATEGY, DETERRENCE AND EUROPEAN SECURITY. 1982. 14pp. $1.00.

FIFTH GERMAN-AMERICAN ROUNDTABLE ON NATO: THE CHANGING CONTEXT OF THE EUROPEAN SECURITY DEBATE. Summary of a Transatlantic Dialogue. 1982. 22pp. $1.00.

ENERGY SECURITY AND THE FUTURE OF NUCLEAR POWER. 1982. 39pp. $2.50.

INTERNATIONAL SECURITY DIMENSIONS OF SPACE. The Eleventh Annual Conference, sponsored by the International Security Studies Program, The Fletcher School of Law and Diplomacy, Tufts University. 1982. 24pp. $2.50.

PORTUGAL, SPAIN AND TRANSATLANTIC RELATIONS. Summary of a Transatlantic Dialogue. 1983. 18pp. $2.50.

JAPANESE-AMERICAN SYMPOSIUM ON REDUCING STRATEGIC MINERALS VULNERABILITIES: CURRENT PLANS, PRIORITIES, AND POSSIBILITIES FOR COOPERATION. 1983. 31pp. $2.50.

NATIONAL SECURITY POLICY: THE DECISION-MAKING PROCESS. The Twelfth Annual Conference, sponsored by the International Security Studies Program, The Fletcher School of Law and Diplomacy, Tufts University. 1983. 28pp. $2.50.

THE SECURITY OF THE ATLANTIC, IBERIAN AND NORTH AFRICAN REGIONS. Summary of a Transatlantic Dialogue. 1983. 25pp. $2.50.

THE WEST EUROPEAN ANTINUCLEAR PROTEST MOVEMENT: IMPLICATIONS FOR WESTERN SECURITY. Summary of a Transatlantic Dialogue. 1984. 21pp. $2.50.

THE U.S.-JAPANESE SECURITY RELATIONSHIP IN TRANSITION. Summary of a Transpacific Dialogue. 1984. 23pp. $2.50.

SIXTH GERMAN-AMERICAN ROUNDTABLE ON NATO: NATO AND EUROPEAN SECURITY—BEYOND INF. Summary of a Transatlantic Dialogue. 1984. 31pp. $2.50.

SECURITY COMMITMENTS AND CAPABILITIES: ELEMENTS OF AN AMERICAN GLOBAL STRATEGY. The Thirteenth Annual Conference, sponsored by the International Security Studies Program, The Fletcher School of Law and Diplomacy, Tufts University. 1984. 21pp. $2.50.

THIRD JAPANESE-AMERICAN-GERMAN CONFERENCE ON THE FUTURE OF NUCLEAR ENERGY. 1984. 40pp. $2.50.

SEVENTH GERMAN-AMERICAN ROUNDTABLE ON NATO: POLITICAL CONSTRAINTS, EMERGING TECHNOLOGIES, AND ALLIANCE STRATEGY. Summary of a Transatlantic Dialogue. 1985. 36pp. $2.50.

TERRORISM AND OTHER "LOW-INTENSITY" OPERATIONS: INTERNATIONAL LINKAGES. The Fourteenth Annual Conference, sponsored by the International Security Studies Program, The Fletcher School of Law and Diplomacy, Tufts University. 1985. 21pp. $2.50.

EAST-WEST TRADE AND TECHNOLOGY TRANSFER: NEW CHALLENGES FOR THE UNITED STATES. Second Annual Forum, co-sponsored by the Institute for Foreign Policy Analysis and the International Security Studies Program, The Fletcher School of Law and Diplomacy, Tufts University. 1986. 40pp. $3.50.

ORGANIZING FOR NATIONAL SECURITY: THE ROLE OF THE JOINT CHIEFS OF STAFF. 1986. 32pp. $2.50.

EIGHTH GERMAN-AMERICAN ROUNDTABLE ON NATO: STRATEGIC DEFENSE, NATO MODERNIZATION, AND EAST-WEST RELATIONS. Summary of a Transatlantic Dialogue. 1986. 47pp. $2.50.

EMERGING DOCTRINES AND TECHNOLOGIES: IMPLICATIONS FOR GLOBAL AND REGIONAL POLITICAL-MILITARY BALANCES. The Fifteenth Annual Conference, sponsored by the International Security Studies Program, The Fletcher School of Law and Diplomacy, Tufts University. 1986. 49pp. $2.50.

STRATEGIC WAR TERMINATION: POLITICAL-MILITARY-DIPLOMATIC DIMENSIONS. 1986. 22pp. $2.50.

STAFFORD LIBRARY
COLUMBIA COLLEGE
1001 ROGERS STREET
COLUMBIA, MO 65216